EPIPHANIES

EPIPHANIES

EPIPHANIES
LIFE CHANGING ENCOUNTERS WITH MUSIC

EDITED BY
TONY HERRINGTON

First published by Strange Attractor Press 2015
© The authors/*The Wire* magazine

ISBN: 9978-1-907222-21-4

All texts previously appeared in *The Wire* magazine
Cover and interior images by Reuben Sutherland
Book design by Ben Weaver

Strange Attractor Press
BM SAP, London, WC1N 3XX, UK
www.strangeattractor.co.uk

WIRE
The Wire
23 Jack's Place, Corbet Place, London E1 6NN, UK
www.thewire.co.uk

Printed in the UK

CONTENTS

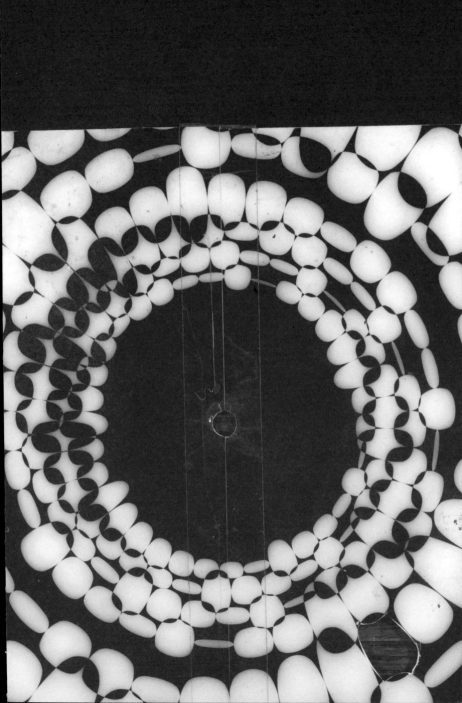

INTRODUCTION

Music changes lives — and here's the proof.

The monthly Epiphanies column which has been running in *The Wire* magazine since January 1998 celebrates music's transformative power in a series of personal testimonials from a wide variety of critics, authors, artists and musicians. This book anthologises 52 of the best Epiphanies essays, each one describing an encounter with a musical event which permanently altered the reality of the writer.

Epiphanies, sonorous or otherwise, come in many forms. They can be instant or elliptical, numinous or traumatic, sensual or philosophical, or all these things and more. They recalibrate the world and illuminate routes to other ways of being.

All the epiphanies described here relate moments of insight or formative experience in ways that resonate universally, attesting to music's ability to cut across time and space in order to clarify thought and alter perception, banish doubt and affirm identity — to change lives.

Tony Herrington
Editor-in-Chief & Publisher
The Wire
6 January 2015

LITTLE ANNIE BANDEZ ON THE RHYTHMS AND BLUES OF NEW YORK

I cannot remember a time that I was not in love with New York. Standing on the corner of our block, I would spend hours gazing south, where its majestically jagged skyline was clearly visible through hazy grey and orange light, like a silhouette of a cheesecake starlet in a Frederick's of Hollywood negligee behind a gauzy curtain. A monochromatic Emerald City, looming full of promise and mystery, it penetrated my very being.

The city was literally on the verge of collapse, yet all its problems made it more attractive to me. The perpetual bad boy and untameable rogue, a sneering juvenile delinquent. If New York were a man, it would be Frank Sinatra with a Lucky Strike behind his ear singing 'Night And Day', phrased with the poise of a drunken tightrope walker who lacks a fear of death. Just when you think the notes will tumble into a heap of broken bones, it swoons into a perfect somersault, surefooted and perfectly focused.

Yes, if New York were a man I'd marry it.

The thing is, lately I've had to accept the fact that this city, that implanted itself so firmly in my heart long ago, is gone, and I find myself in the arms of an impostor.

In the mid-1970s this town was busted. Crime-ridden, in impossible debt and going to hell in a shoplifted handbag. We knew we were going to hell because the daily news told us so. The infamous headline, 'FORD TO CITY: DROP DEAD', appeared in 1975. Little by little, the powers that be, in desperation, must have taken to heart the quote (attributed to an anonymous US military officer in Vietnam in 1968), 'It became necessary to destroy the town to save it.' There was no need for typhoid-spiked blankets, just real estate agents. They cured the illness but killed the patient.

Of course there are a few of us holdouts, steadfast be it from idealism or bitterness or, like myself, blinded by love. But we are quickly becoming cigar store Indians, a multi-hued diminishing tribe of subway samurai: we mimic ourselves

15

as we were portrayed in the movies, tough talking, cigar chomping Broadway Bennies, armed with zip guns, borscht belt wit and hearts of gold (and that's just the women!). When us diehards die out, we will be like the Aztecs, taking our culture into the afterlife with us.

I am in love with a ghost.

Still, love is foolish, and despite its egregious betrayal of its past, its nose job, orange spray tan and, worst of all, its West Coast dumb girl vocabulary — 'Like, ya know, like, like...' — I cannot help but think that underneath, in its heart (that is, if it still has one), there is a battered, limping, beautiful hipster trying desperately to bust loose.

About ten years ago, while out of town with a bad bout of homesickness, I listened non-stop to the Miles Davis album *Kind Of Blue*, and only that, for at least a month. In the haunting joy and longing, I heard a lifetime, not just my own, but that of all who walked along the Bosphorus gold of the Hudson River, lost in the magic of a multi-hued dusk, as the slightest of breezes brings a gentle drop of relief at the end of a red hot and grimy day.

Once again I find myself homesick, even while staring out my window that looks onto midtown Manhattan. And as Miles blows 'Blue In Green', 'So What' or 'Freddie Freeloader', or any of that genius wordless narrative, my brain's eye runs a soft focus filmstrip of an arrogantly innocent New York, wounded and proud, like Icarus reaching for heights it probably has no business reaching for, but does so regardless. Chinatown, with its impossible golds and clashing pinks and reds, where my quiet opiated daydreams reside among piles of fish, plastic flowers and thousand year old secrets. The pedestrians, basking or scrambling in the seizure-shadows as the subway rattles over the El over the concourse near the Gunhill Road in the Bronx. The old money/Art Deco understated beige that the rich paint their apartments, in which they live invisible lives and are served dinner by butlers in front of curtainless windows in full view of the commuters snaking up FDR Drive, which is turned by rush hour from the Indianapolis 500 into a snail track. The sunset browns, violets and oranges of Harlem, where each building is of a different architectural style than the one next to it, making it a paramour that will never cease being mysterious. Lower Manhattan, where the avenues had a nervous breakdown, becoming sharply diagonal and illogical. Central Park, lounging like a plump lethargic lady in a green velvet dress, who is tired from too much shopping, and just plunked herself down in the very middle of a busy thoroughfare and stubbornly decided to stay. The Essex House where the the angel-throated Donny Hathaway, burdened by genius and schizophrenia, no longer able to withstand the hurt, jumped to his death and lay undiscovered till morning. God's Kitchen, at the turn-off to the Pulaski Bridge that joins two boroughs, making them first cousins. Cole Porter's piano turned resplendent, a silent shrine behind a velvet rope. The stretch of Eighth Avenue between 34th and 40th Street, which stubbornly remains, as it has always been, a citadel under attack (this time around from vague young things with coy square eyes, mobile phones and a bad grasp of history). The metal skeleton sentries that dig their rusty heels in the sooty shores of the Harlem River.

In the voodoo eyes and melancholy blue notes of the final trumpet played by the jilted jazzman on his way to heaven, I see my beloved's face...

Little Annie Bandez, aka Annie Anxiety, is a US singer, songwriter, performer and visual artist

The room is pretty much bare, just a chair, some rudimentary
equipment. From the window you can see the church clock
down the road. The town sprawls out every which way,
lapsing into incoherence where the railway abandons it
by the side of the shanty-lined road. The place is Grafton,
Wisconsin and it is February 1931. The man who climbs the
stairs and takes the chair is Nehemiah 'Skip' James, who has
come there to play music. He's there a few days, perhaps,
sleeping in a cheap room on the other side of town. He has
signed to lay down some race records for Mr HC Spier. The
two men meet twice and James, who has been to divinity
school, signs his name on Spier's contract at their second
and final meeting. He's 28 years old, a loner whose God is
neither jealous nor vengeful, but rather a little odd.

His music is uncanny; a dramatic and audibly weird
combination of guitar licks executed with lightning speed
and a ghostly voice that comes directly from another world.
There's humour in the voice, just, but its tone is more
palpably alarming. A high keening voice that makes the
fields, the church, the forest and the railroad yard its own.
Transcendent is a term that history will apply to this music
when half a lifetime later it is picked up by rock groups
hungry to mine its meanings. Some of Skip's songs become
classics long after they have been forgotten by the audience
they were made for. His lyrics strike a note of batty euphoria
that impresses itself on the teenager's brain. *'I'm so glad, I am
glad, I am glad, I'm glad. I don't know what to do, don't know
what to do, don't know what to do'*. His inimitable, fluid guitar
playing is imitated by the great and the good and towards
the end of his life he even makes some money from it. He's
located in a hospital bed, brought to a few folk festivals in
his final years. But the disjointed, happy accident that brings
the spotlight spinning crazily over him in old age is as of
nothing compared to that which is given voice in the wintry
room in Grafton.

18 songs survive, five with Skip playing piano, for the rest he's on the guitar. He sounds like he's enjoying himself. But his voice carries such contradictory messages. At times he's in agony, screeching in pain. Hysteria never seems too far away; he's energised, now wacky, then scarily dark. His songs are waiting for electricity; they bide their time in a state of restlessness. Their violence is of the broody sort. No music, perhaps, sits so strangely with its form.

By virtue of their rarity Skip's surviving recordings are all badly scratched acetates. One in particular, 'Four O'Clock Blues', comprises 50 per cent Skip, 50 per cent surface noise. When I first heard it, I laughed that anyone should bother to rerelease it. Closer listening, and a growing conviction that if you assume that what an artist does is — or necessarily appears to be — conscious, led me to come back again and again to this song. Its fascinations expanded in a hallucinatory fugue which I grew to love. We hear him in a hailstorm, in the lumber yard with its saws buzzing, on a goods train, in the deafening machine room down from the tin mine. Is he screaming in rage or agony? Is his soul railing against the grinding wheel of the hand-to-mouth life of the Depression? Or is he laughing madly as the press churns out its absurd, off-kilter parody of these few minutes from his life? It remains impenetrable.

While Charley Patton was adept enough to toy with the recording process, even in the early days of the blues, and while Son House ignored its restrictions, running his songs over both sides of the acetate, James seems to be half-listening to that scratching sound, wondering perhaps how to live with it. The materiality of the recording has its own rhythms, its own aesthetic life, and even as he sings he is aware that it is burying him. If we can imagine that beneath the inaudible lyrics and shattered guitar picking it's a fairly standard song, the years have yet stretched away and pulled a weird punch so that, at times, 'Four O'Clock Blues' haphazardly prefigures musique concrète. As reality is swallowed by loopy myth, as each gesture of the player is transfigured in the fire of the listener's imagination, so this record seems to be drawing energy into its impenetrable black heart. We see it on a shelf somewhere, too dark to make out, like something from a Marvel comic strip, something evil and bossily menacing. We see it in a museum store, waiting with the patience of the dead for time to pass: each second that goes by makes it more meaningful but we can't yet say why. Knowledge retreats into a baffling parody of guilt as we wear away the object, even as we attempt to fathom its depths.

I shut up, aware of failure. I hallucinate as I listen. The grooves in this record, the sole copy of which slips through the war and secretes itself in a safe hiding place for another quarter of a century, rise before me like an Iron Age fort in the gulleys of which I, a child, run shrieking my head off from joy, or fear. Night closes in and I'm waiting for the headache, for the hangover, an undertaker or for daybreak. In the gloom I run through the steps that lead to my one shot at a second take, the chance to slake my thirst at the enormous tit of some impish muse.

The recording bisects Skip's life. Born in 1902, dead in 1969, did he ever hear it back, even once? He moved on, working in the mines, travelling, falling ill on the plantation down in Tunica where John Fahey and his friends sought him out. As though time could be cheated. Once instinct with life, the records had all disappeared, into attics, junk shops, thrown out with the trash. A group of kids find a pile in some flyblown basement and later they are seen in the street chucking them at the side of a firehouse, where they explode in loud, clear laughter. One throws a copy at a stray dog and it shatters to pieces as the creature backs away down a cluttered, dreary alley.

In the bare room above the store we watch the hands of the clock as the February afternoon drags on. The sunlight changes rapidly, there's a storm about to break, so that each take seems bathed in both night and day. The minute hand hits 12 and for a moment time implodes, sucks in sharply before exhaling clouds of dust, tattered leaves, rotten wardrobes, bones as white as a blind man's stick, vast rafts of clotted blood, layers of what we momentarily recognise as history. The machine is ready. The man in the felt hat and cheap suit gives him the nod, stubs out his cigarette, picks at his ear lobe without knowing. Then the player picks up the guitar and strikes the strings.

Ed Baxter is Programming Director of the UK arts and community radio station Resonance104.4fm

It was a different world back then. It seems to me there was less of everything. Certainly less music. And what music there was came out of small radios. Or the enormous piano in the corner of the living room. To me, sitting underneath it as a child, the piano seemed vast, but in fact it was between a grand and a baby grand, a size termed a Boudoir, and I've never seen one since.

I grew up playing the flute in a remote Sussex village, in a house without any electricity. By day I tended a small herd of goats on the hillside, and improvised on the piccolo while ambling through fields of barley. OK, I made up the goats, but my point is that my exposure to either live or recorded music was minuscule until I arrived at college, in Cambridge, 1969. Here I was knocked sideways by an epiphanic series of concerts and encounters. Jethro Tull — the showmanship and sheer volume, the knowing humour and musicianship, something like Ian Dury's Blockheads ten years later. Pink Floyd — Syd Barrett had just left, and they spun a sonic maelstrom round our heads, threatening to suck us all in. Karlheinz Stockhausen came to town and lectured about something similar. And The Incredible String Band played again and again, shambling across the stage between 50 unnameable instruments, taking an age between numbers because someone had to tune the zither played by Licorice — was she the one that later became Mayor of Taunton?

But we always forgave The String Band everything, because their music was subtle and whimsical, and because they embodied so many alternatives, so many rejections of things that had seemed important before. For example, that you must impress the audience with technical expertise (jazz), and you must play aggressive and loud (rock). These genre conventions were OK up to a point, and we all enjoyed a visit from Detroit's MC5 — like the self-flagellating initiates of an exhausting cult, they pounded out rock's underlying mystery till we were almost too numb to applaud. But the best groups defied these conventions, rewrote the rules, and were of course derided by many disappointed music fans.

Notorious among Cambridge's homegrown groups was Henry Cow. Tim Hodgkinson (sax and organ) and Fred Frith (guitar) had originally formed a six piece dada blues group, but by the time I saw them, the blues standards had moved to the encore list, and Henry Cow were a trio playing their own complex chamber rock compositions. John Greaves, a bass player with a fondness for the upper reaches of the instrument, had joined; he also liked to sing the odd Frank Sinatra tribute. The group's reputation preceded them, in the sense that they annoyed the hell out of several people I knew. It was rock music of a sort, but there was no drummer, and they played sitting down. An exciting riff would appear, only to be dismissed after four bars in favour of a Webernian atonal melody in 13/8 time. No proper guitar solos, but melodies on the bass and abrasive improvising on sax. Instead of liquid slides and strobe lights, a tasselled standard lamp on stage. And a man ironing his clothes throughout the set.

I think the combination of playful and serious attracted me straight away. This was an honest music too, in that no one was posing or following a US rock style book. You didn't have to leave your brain in the dressing room, and the music told you that an interest in Messiaen and Hendrix might be compatible. You have to remember this was before progressive rock, which always seemed to be about musicians who had had a lot of classical piano lessons and wanted to pump it up on stage in the overblown manner of Berlioz's *Symphonie Fantastique*. Henry Cow were more about questioning the separation of 20th century composition and rock, set in a context of happenings, psychedelia and street theatre. Becoming friends with this group made college life considerably more interesting. By this time my patience with Roman history seminars was wearing thin. I had a nasty case of mumps, which got me isolated in a hospital room, a small mirror on the opposite wall; I was told not to move my back. I also took part in performances of a Greek comedy, staged in ancient Greek of course, for which I played Frank Zappa-style flute music while suspended high above the stage, dressed as a bird, in a gently swaying cage. By the end of a week of this, I was staggering everywhere, affected by motion sickness and nausea.

I started playing occasionally with Henry Cow, when there was room in the van. Fred Frith showed considerable generosity, or recklessness, by inviting me on stage for an improvised set when we hadn't even been properly introduced. He also played me a recording of Toru Takemitsu's *November Steps*, and so I heard the sound of the shakuhachi for the first time. Meanwhile, Henry Cow searched for a drummer. Several were tried, but a remarkable musician was needed to render convincingly those constantly varying time signatures and tempi. And so it came to pass that Chris Cutler was auditioned (in 1972) and got the job, and I was excited to be present. Cutler announced he liked the group's 'row', and immediately propelled them onto another level, a more extrovert mode of performance, maybe more accessible. 13/8 was meat and drink to Cutler, as was free improvising; and being suitably opinionated, he slotted well into the fierce debating society that the group became once offstage.

But did Henry Cow lose something by appointing a drummer? The first LP, *Legend*, was recorded with Cutler in 1973. Those pre-1972 concerts had a weird but warm chamber quality that I've never heard in another group. All three instruments had to state the complex rhythms with no percussive help. And then there's the febrile excitement of hearing a group early on, before they've really discovered what it is they do. Drummer or no drummer, the rock press gave Henry Cow a hard time, usually by fastidiously ignoring them. As Hanif Kureishi wrote, pop music is 'a form crying out not to be written about'. Some rock critics seemed to despise themselves for writing at all, and compensated by adopting a virile anti-intellectualism. Groups like Soft Machine and Henry Cow received a warmer welcome in Europe, where maybe there was less sense of shame at enjoying complex composition, improvisation and blues all at the same time. Or possibly they were suckers for pretentious nonsense? Whatever, I felt that an England with a bit more cultural self-confidence, a bit less kowtowing to American models, would have taken Henry Cow more to its heart, would have been proud of producing something so odd and multi-coloured.

Clive Bell is a UK musician and music critic

I didn't know what I was hearing at first, a big kind of static
roar, full of bass, ripples of distortion. It sounded like a
drone, but where was it coming from? The TV was on in my
living room in downtown Toronto, it was the summer of
2010 and the World Cup had started. I don't have cable, so
I'm used to getting a crappy signal, and at first I put it down
to static or some kind of sonic distortion. Sort of cool still,
but whatever. Then, like everyone, I started reading about
vuvuzelas, cheap plastic single-tone trumpets that South
African fans attending the games blew on to create a wall of
sound. I started to listen more carefully and came to savour
that wall of sound, also getting off on the way that it was
driving a lot of other people crazy, in much the same way that
drone music seems to.

What was it, really, that we were hearing when we
listened to the vuvuzelas? I came to think of it, perhaps
naively, as the sound of the global South, the buzzing
hive sound of the people of the world, contaminating the
otherwise clean hyperspace of the globalised spectacle
of soccer, now trademarked and sold to us by FIFA. A
reminder that you can't send a message without distortion
entering in, and that if you listen to the messages of
global capital, they will always be accompanied by their
subaltern support, the global multitude. Just as I love
the way that drones piss people off, I loved the appalled
reaction of many commentators to the vuvuzelas, and the
calls for these trumpets and the drones they created to be
banned. Apparently, the mere sonic presence of the people
in the curated space of the contemporary sports stadium
constituted a disturbance that had to be managed through
public health discourses that included not only claims
that vuvuzelas could cause serious hearing loss, but more
remarkably, that they could spread flu viruses and other
contagious diseases.

To me, it was also a reminder that drone music is not

a technique invented by the minimalist avant gardes, but one of the sounds of the people, spanning a very broad historical and geographical continuum, from the biblical horn that blew Jericho down to the OM that gave birth to the universe in the Hindu scriptures, on to all the various folk musics that rely on sustained tones. Drone music is easily configured as a collective technique, if only because playing sustained tones together is a simple method of amplification in a non-electronic culture — for example, Tibetan Buddhist monasteries, where monks blow massive mountain horns simultaneously to produce the raw blast of sound that invites the deities to the ritual.

But the sound also reminded me of something more specific. A few months before, I had started a monthly club night called MAMA in Toronto with a few friends, dedicated to what we called global psychedelic dancehall. I had been reading blogs such as DJ /rupture's Mudd Up or the encylopedic Generation Bass for a while, and also just finished Steve Goodman's *Sonic Warfare*, which ends with an amazing analysis of the power of bass music made in the shanty towns of the world, from São Paulo to Soweto to the Parisian banlieues. I was immersed in Brazilian baile funk, the post-Nortec Tijuana scene, Angolan kuduro, cumbia from Argentina, Colombia, Mexico, Germany; hiphop, dubstep from all over. And then there was the Syrian singer Omar Souleyman, who I got to see in the summer of 2008 in Berlin, playing his astounding techno-dabke fusion, full of noisy distorted bass and percussion and that incredible rasping voice.

But what really stole my heart as I experimented each month in putting things together was South African house or kwaito. We were all swimming deep in the ocean of sound, but one night my friend Dorian confided that when people ask him what he's into, he just says, 'I love house.' And I came to feel that way too. The tune that kills me is JR's 'Show Dem', a big hit in South Africa in 2010. And it is this track in particular that reminded me of those vuvuzelas. It's house music, with that familiar heartbeat bass drum, but then after about 30 seconds, the bass comes in with an enormous drone-like farting thickness that sputters off into noise and distortion at the edges, almost like the drum 'n' bass tracks issued in the 1990s by the UK No U-Turn label, but somehow more turbulent and sensuous. I came to relish that moment every time I DJed because it so reliably destroyed dancefloors as well as putting serious pressure on the relatively cheap sub bins at Teranga, the Senegalese nightclub at which MAMA happened.

Steve Goodman is justifiably cautious about appropriating these sounds into a Hardt and Negri-style fantasy of the global multitude. I try to learn something about the music I play, but often all I have is a barely labelled sound file, and if it kills on the dancefloor, that's OK. I don't know how to justify my interest or participation in this music except to say that I am a thief among thieves, and I do it out of love and because I don't know what else to do. I don't know much about JR. When I hear the voices on SA house tracks such as those on the remarkable *Ayobaness!* compilation, or baile funk or kuduro, I'm reminded of the carnivalesque vocal polyphony of early hiphop in New York, or, for that matter, hiphop wherever it remains vital. To me it sounds like the people having a conversation, and that's something I like to hear, precisely because it's so unclear who 'the people' are today. But there's no simple equation between music, class, ethnicity and authenticity. And often it's outsiders or interlopers who make connections that others can't or don't.

I love the journey that house has made from black gay clubs in Chicago and New York in the 1970s and 80s to South Africa, where, at the moment apartheid ended in the early 1990s, kwaito was born as a strange electronic mutation of house and hiphop with SA pop styles such as mbqanga. I like the thought of Moodymann and Ten City being played in the townships. I know that house is also the music of the global shopping mall and the high street boutique. I imagine that I can tell the difference, and that JR's farting bass would disqualify him from French Connection or the duty free store at Heathrow, but I'm not sure. What I do know is that there is something like a sound of freedom, which happens when people are talking to each other with whatever comes to hand. It may take a little time but, as with the vuvuzela, we can learn to recognise it.

Marcus Boon is Professor of English at Toronto's York University

For over 30 years, too much has been said about John Cage's notion of 'silence'. I first encountered Cage in 1975 — my formative year. While listening extensively to prog, krautrock, glam, disco, Stravinsky, Schoenberg and Stockhausen, my interest in the musical polarities of heightened surface and sonic density broadened my aural perception and made me aware of obtuse interconnections in supposedly disparate musics. Conversely, I heard next to no Cage that year, but read his *Silence* (1961), Richard Kostelanetz's *John Cage* (1970) and Calvin Tomkins's *Ahead Of The Game* (1965). I thought Cage might provide insight into my 'conflicted' listening. Although enthused by the concept of widening one's listening range to accept all sounds, I could not get past the haiku-tinged, wispy 'love of life' aphorisms mottling these books. Fortunately, the Cage music I heard the following year imparted greater moments, from the delicate prepared piano of *Sonatas & Interludes* (1946–48) to the overloaded sono-media collage of *Fontana Mix* (1958). Yet while many other writers, composers and artists I encountered also seemed attracted to his thoughts, Cage's Easternised philosophising didn't appeal to me, high as I was at the time on Duchamp's wilfully perverse articulation of a meta-practice of art and Warhol's theatrical denial of any art practice.

Cage — or precisely, the presentation of Cage back then — irritated me with its 'a-culturalism', the way his 'indeterminate' compositional strategies removed the work from any cultural specificity. This irritation acted on two levels: firstly via its locus in the rarefied domain of experimental music practice and its influence on Fluxus's alignment with the art gallery — realms where composer directive and artist statement overrode any sociocultural framing of their outcomes. Secondly, through the reduction of 'sound' to a quasi-mystical zone where 'sound itself' speaks most eloquently of its substance and existence. From the precious privilege born of the former to the vacuous view endeared by the latter, the appreciation of Cage seemed delineated by its own anechoic

chamber which excluded the world and its cultural noise —
all while deftly reducing it to an amorphous voluminous
mass. It was as if all sound was to be celebrated — so long as it
wasn't labelled, categorised or named.

If this were a standard epiphany, we would now move
on to how something revolutionised my misreading of Cage.
That never happened, nor is it likely — so Cage enthusiasts
may maintain that I am continuing this misreading.
Proportionately, Cage tends to be lionised more as time goes
by — indeed, as if time remains frozen. The critical ground
for Cage has undoubtedly produced many great works, but
'a-culturalism' still embalms their didactic spread: much
of that work could be excitingly recouped not by returning
to their mythological originations as artworks, but by
considering them unpatronisingly in tandem with all other
forms of sound and music happening in their time. Such
an option would move us not to a thin understanding of
'sound' but a maximised register of 'music'. 'Sound' — via its
purported expansiveness and inclusivity in opposition to a
presumably outmoded notion of 'music' — is still invoked
today in experimental music circles as if it is pure, real,
natural, truthful — I can hardly type such words without my
brain hurting.

Similarly, the mere utterance of 'the beautiful' — despite
its Zen slant inferred by Cage's lectures, talks and interviews
— is still deemed to be an escape hatch to a 'de-critiqued' zone.
There are many contemporary musicians and composers —
from the realm of academic turrets to the subterranean sewers
of avant rock — who talk of a redefined beauty in sound, and
their views are thereby inflected with a foppish, affected
amour des arts. The idea that 'sound' is somehow the essence
of musicality is a concept as sentimental as the conclusion of
Lord Of The Rings.

Many years after my high school encounter with Cage,
I saw the 1990 PBS documentary *I Have Nothing To Say
And I Am Saying It*. It précised all to be expected of Cage,
alongside a number of alarmingly unqualified assertions
by learned others of his great contribution to 20th century
music. Again, I was struck by how time was still frozen. Again

I was flummoxed by the narrow gauge of critical discourse generated from such supposedly all-encompassing life celebrating concepts.

But just as I was disengaging myself from the journalistic accolades of this documentary, the programme shifts to a rehearsal and presentation of *Speech* (1955) — one of Cage's composed actions for radios, here staged in 1982 at the Symphony Space, New York. Again, it's one of those works that sounds better on paper than it sounds itself — which is Cageian, I guess. But this time, we're in New York during the stirrings of hiphop. As the performers shift the dials, funky breaks, electro beats and disco divas materialise in this symphonic space. Maybe in early multimedia performances such as *Radio Music* (1956), Jerry Lee Lewis and Joe Turner ruptured those premieres with their musical identities — but no writer of the time would have had the acumen to trace the intercultural connectivity of noise making in both. Cage's essays, plus many writers on his work, are alarmingly dismissive of post-Second World War American mass culture. The problem is that no writing since has evidenced such connectivity of cultural voices which generate the noise that allows Cage and those influenced by him to, through contradistinction, espouse notions of 'silence'.

This is not to denigrate the Cage legacy: it will persist. If I had written this in 1975, it would have the same punk flippancy it retains more than 30 years later.

If anything, the shortcomings in applying Cage's ideas to a pluralist cultural domain have conversely allowed me the freedom to declare no fundamental difference between Gary Glitter's 'Rock And Roll' and Stockhausen's *Kontakte*. I've since perceived that the abject acoustica of even the most vapid music can sometimes betray an overwhelming depth of 'sound itself' in contrast to the pumped-up self-mythologising that passes for the bulk of so-called radical sound art practice. The PBS documentary without prescience documented precisely what hiphop was doing in channels of production beyond this Cage performance. Seminal 'sonic energisers' Terminator X and Hank Shocklee were arguably more Cageian than Cage in their embrace of the overload

of sound, noise and music in the urban noisescape, plus
their music 'sounds itself' at the praxis of technology, folk,
industry and art. Watching this documentary in 1990 — some
time after Public Enemy's radical yet populist call to noise
— as four people feebly twiddled radios between stations,
the shards of music I heard ironically proved one of Cage's
seminal and liberating ideas: there is so much more beyond
the concert hall.

Philip Brophy is an Australian musician, film maker, critic and curator

SAMANTHA BROWN ON THE LESSON BOB DYLAN
LEARNED FROM A SONG BY A GIRL FROM THE NORTH
COUNTRY

Cover versions are a two edged sword. In the wrong hands
they can be a horribly messy business. As a notoriously erratic
performing artist, Bob Dylan has never needed outside
help getting his hands messy. Through prolonged periods
of the so-called Never Ending Tour he launched in 1988, he
has come across as a baleful, driven presence, not so much
struggling with inner demons as his own boredom with
having to pick himself up from the floor and slug his way
through a body of work that no longer enchanted him the
way it evidently still did his audience. Up until the mid-1990s,
he frequently sang as though he was sick of the sound of his
own voice, or at least the way it bounced back at him from his
more fanatical followers' adulation.

Contrary as ever, the sick at heart troubadour, seemingly
alienated from the most significant canon of the 20th century,
began supplementing his set with cover versions drawn from a
songbook ranging between centuries-old folk songs, haunting
mountain bluegrass spirituals and the cheesiest MOR ballads.
Very soon these became set highlights — sometimes if only for
the sheer perversity of hearing Dylan croak-croon 'Help Me
Make It Through The Night', for instance. Not only has he
been less cavalier in his performances of material other than
his own, but also he has been rediscovering his voice these
past 15 years by inhabiting those of other writers. And of the
200-odd — some of them extremely odd — songs Dylan has
covered over the duration of his Never Ending Tour, one in
particular, called 'Oh Babe It Ain't No Lie', moved me enough
to track it back to its source.

The first time Dylan performed it — during his NET
run, at least — in January 1990 at an uncharacteristically
upbeat four hour warm-up concert for its latest leg, at Toad's
Place, New Haven, he threw himself on the blades of a dozen
covers and miraculously emerged from them all unscathed.
If the same couldn't be said for all the songs, however, Dylan

reserved a special tenderness for the hurt yet defiant lyric and easily bruised melody of 'Oh Babe It Ain't No Lie'. As a vessel for a Dylan performance, a song about lying and its painful consequences is not in itself a surprise. Trying to figure out what it was in his voice that wouldn't let go threw me back on one of Dylan's own great lying songs, this time the studio take of a Dylan original, 'Idiot Wind', from his 1975 masterpiece *Blood On The Tracks*. And for sure, the opening lines of both songs bear a fleeting resemblance.

'*One old woman Lord in this town*', sings Dylan at Toad's Place, '*Keeps a-telling her lies on me/Wish to my soul that old woman would die/Keep a-telling her lies on me/Oh babe it ain't no lie* [×3]/*Know this life I'm living is very high*'. 'Idiot Wind' opens from a not dissimilar corner: '*Someone's got it in for me, they're planting stories in the press/Whoever it is I wish they'd cut it out quick, but when they will I can only guess*'.

Both vocals are profoundly affecting yet the difference between them in tone couldn't be more marked. In the first, the singer is curled up in the corner, in the other he comes out fighting. It's only after tracking down the original 'Oh Babe It Ain't No Lie' to Elizabeth Cotten's 1958 Folkways album *Freight Train And Other North Carolina Folk Songs And Tunes*, and hearing its composer perform it, that it began to make sense.

Born in 1892, as a young girl the left handed Cotten taught herself to play banjo and guitar upside down, a method through which she devised her influential folk and ragtime blues picking. Her playing was later identified as a North Carolina picking style akin to Reverend Gary Davis and Mississippi John Hurt when she began sharing bills with them on folk and blues stages in the 1960s. That she got to play with them at all is not without irony as, God-fearing to a fault, Cotten had pretty much given up playing for 40 years after her church condemned secular music as the devil's plaything. Indeed she only began playing again when she picked up a guitar in the household of the famous folk family the Seegers, where she worked as a domestic help, and Mike Seeger coaxed her into recording the pieces she remembered adapting and writing as a girl.

On a live album recorded in the late 1970s, by which time she was in her eighties, she described the gestation of 'Oh Babe It Ain't No Lie': 'Now the story behind that, the old lady caused my mother to punish me because she's told my mother I sassed her and I didn't. And momma kept me inside the house... It hurt my feelings because the woman, Miss Mary, I liked her very much and to think she would tell momma something, momma punish me, and I lay in bed at night and cry right easy and I made this little verse up about her and I'd sit on the end of my porch and play it and sing it as loud as I could, and she would say to me, 'That certainly is a pretty song, what is it, Sis?' And I wanted to say, Miss Mary it's about you, but I couldn't tell her that because I'd have got punished again. Miss Mary died and she didn't know this song was about her. Momma died and she didn't know what it is about either. Now I'm gonna play it all I want for y'all.'

So here's a woman disarmingly evoking, from the distance and wisdom of 40 and more years, all the anger and defiance her young girl self could muster. And here's Dylan singing the same song three years after the woman who wrote it died (she was 92), singing her young self's song, as projected through the mature Cotten's version. And it suddenly becomes clear that here's a song that cannot be sung in any other voice or from any other perspective than its author's. The process of honouring the song by singing it in Cotten's voice, without lapsing into a form of vocal transvestism, taught Dylan something missing from his own angry hurt vehicles: tolerance and vulnerability.

Samantha Brown never lived in Bob Dylan's house for about four or five months

The autumn of 1974 was not a particularly great time for
music. If you don't believe me, look it up. During that bleak
season, however, a musical bomb exploded in my face,
reordering my way of thinking for all time.

This metamorphosis occurred in the television studio
at Hampshire College. As a wannabe video artist, I had
signed up for a class called Performing and Recording Arts
Workshop, taught by a somewhat weedy itinerant professor
named John Gray. On this afternoon, John had promised
us 'something special', and the class assembled in the close
confines of Studio A. The lights went out and John told us
he was going to play a piece of music by one of the students,
Robbie Carey. He cued the class's student aide, Ken 'Mr Jazz'
Burns (I shit you not), to roll the tape. Anticipation built for
a few seconds, then the darkness was rent by a voice that
sounded like Rockette Morton's on Captain Beefheart's *Trout
Mask Replica*:

> 'Save every fish! Save every fish!
> Raven
> Save every fish! Save every fish!
> Raven raven
> The captain is
> Raven raven
> The captain is
> Raven raven
> The captain is
> Entirely wasted'

Jesus, what is going on? There was a cascade of voices in
the darkness. Each of them was ostensibly normal enough,
but their speech patterns had been ripped apart and rebuilt
in a way that rendered them absurd and crazy in the best
surrealist tradition. Behind the voices were snippets of
music that had been sundered in a similar manner. It was

like nothing I had ever heard before; but it wasn't completely random, it had an obviously composed structure. The piece moved through different settings, interspersing repeating series of words with new sets of repeated words in a way that either amplified or destroyed the meaning they carried. As the tape unspooled, it became apparent that the whole carried a whacked rhythmic underpinning that suggested true musicality.

It was as though some evil conceptual art dentist yanked all the teeth out of my head, and pounded them back into different root-maws, singing loopily and banging the mallet in odd, disjointed beats.

The piece was entitled 'Coarse Fish' and hearing it was a complete HOLY SHIT moment for me. This stuff functioned as music, even though it didn't really have any of the components you'd list if someone asked you to explain what music was. It existed in its own unique, fucked up place in the universe, and if it wasn't the purest goddamn ART I'd ever heard, then I didn't know a thing about the subject. I immediately flashed on all kinds of theoretical possibilities for my own work. As I later came to know Robbie, and began to participate in the tape experiments he was conducting as Orchid Spangiafora, the sonic rupturing of 'Coarse Fish' became emblematic of a whole way of thinking, writing and doing. Chaotic hilarity was everywhere. It lurked just below the surface of the most staid stuff imaginable. All it required to be set free was a little teasing. We subsequently spent sodden years investigating this 'theory' via collages, joke deconstructions, strange public activities and drugged recording sessions, which Robbie would splice up and work on for endless hours.

The screwball musical sculptures that he spent so long assembling in the dark confines of the Hampshire Electronic Music Studio were obviously great work, exquisitely wrought. But they were also intensely personal, self-referential and germane only to our circle of friends. It was difficult to conceive of anyone else who might be interested in hearing this babble. Beyond that, if anyone was interested, how would you get the stuff to them? This was a real stumper. The thought that even an oddball label might be interested, like Island or Harvest (the scope of our knowledge of 'oddball' labels in 1974), was beyond the realm of possibility. And no other known options existed. So the Orchid material was presented at infrequent live electronic music recitals and was passed around among a few people on cassette. And that was assumed to be that.

Then came the dawning of punk and everything shifted again. Chris Osgood, another Hampshire student, and a participant in the Orchid sessions, was from Minnesota. He had moved back to the Twin Cities after college, and led a series of groups that evolved into The Suicide Commandos, one of the very first of the punk (or whatever) combos in the Midwest. In 1976, The Commandos (with the help of Paul Stark) issued a single of their own, and that gesture provided another revelatory flash. You could actually put out a record yourself! Who would've thought such a thing was possible? But Chris and Paul knew how to do it, and they were willing to let Robbie in on the secret.

And if you could actually get the record out, then Greg Shaw might write about it in *Bomp*. And Irwin Chusid might play it on his radio show on WFMU. And Hideo's Discodrome might take a few copies to put up next to the new Pere Ubu single. And you could give a copy to Burroughs and... on and on and on. The possibilities were endless and thinking about them was enough to make anyone breathless. No one (at least in the US) had figured out how to get paid, but that wasn't really the point. You could do it. And that was its own reward.

To release your own record was wildly liberating. It brought home one of the great concepts of the punk era (that of the levelling of the unequal relationship between performer and audience) in a most satisfying way. And it exploded the mysteries that surrounded the commodification of art. I mean, making this record (or, really, observing the process by which Robbie had the record made), stripped an entire mystical layer from the work of people we liked, but whose productions seemed so sophisticated and artful as to come from another realm. It became clear that people like The Residents or Devo were, more likely than not, just befuddled bozos like us, who had been able to decode the process a little bit earlier and were, thus, further advanced in terms of packaging.

There were no magic words to be spoken. There were no impossible hurdles to be jumped. It was just a matter of saving enough money and sending the right kinds of tapes and art and stuff to the people who had the machinery to turn this weird, ethereal shit into a commodity. That may have been the biggest epiphany of all. And it began with 'Mr Jazz' hitting the PLAY button in a dark television studio, 28 years ago this month. Wow.

Byron Coley is a US music critic, poet and record dealer

It was a winter of high drama on the boulevards of Belgrade.
The year was 1996, and the government of Slobodan
Milosevic seemed to be on the verge of falling. It had already
led Yugoslavia into the wars that would tear it apart, while
becoming increasingly repressive within the borders of
the republic of Serbia itself. When Milosevic falsified the
results of local elections to keep his supporters in power,
Serbia erupted into civic revolt. Every day, hundreds of
thousands took to the streets in some of the most powerful
and theatrical protests in recent European history. The
sheer sound of it was incredible: a sharp, bright screech of
massed whistles blown in fury, underpinned by the deep,
mournful lowing of cow horns and the jaunty syncopation
of percussion ensembles stepping in rhythm through the
crowds, bashing out a feisty Serbian rumba. 'They exorcised
evil spirits,' one Belgrade writer said at the time. 'They
fought shame with noise.' And when the mendacious state
television news came on air every evening, people would lean
out of their windows simultaneously and batter away on pots
and pans, attempting to blank out the insidious drone of
distortion — drumming for their lives.

It was a time of anger and hope, a time for taking sides,
and music was no exception. If you were into techno or rock
'n' roll, you were probably with the opposition. This was
music that signified the desire to break out of the suffocating
isolation that Milosevic had brought down on Serbia — and
to become part of the world again. It was an implicit rejection
of nationalism. Meanwhile, the state had its own favourite
soundtrack: turbo-folk, a mixture of tinny Europop and
traditional Balkan melodies. Turbo-folk was the music of the
war years, the ethnic cleansing campaigns in Bosnia and the
rise of the Versace-clad gangster profiteers — 'the music of
death', as more than one Belgrade commentator called it. It
was the sound of the militias and the mafia, a danse macabre
to an electronic beat. Its biggest star, Ceca, was married to

41

the hoodlum-turned-warlord Arkan, a union that brought together the cultural and the political, a perfect symbol for those dark times. Arkan would later be shot dead in the lobby of an upmarket hotel, and a few years afterwards, Ceca would be arrested (but ultimately released) in the aftermath of the assassination of prime minister Zoran Djindjic.

Techno had recently arrived in the city, and some would go straight from the protests to the Kozmik parties at the subterranean Industria club. Underground Resistance never sounded so vital. But the dissidents had their own indigenous soundtrack, too; groups who played at the protest rallies and brought the turbulence on the streets into their music. Foremost among them was the punk-funk ensemble Darkwood Dub. Their songs had echoes of A Certain Ratio and Talking Heads, but they were also charged with the kinetic energy of drum 'n' bass, and had the punk rocker's love of reggae.

Reggae was incredibly popular in Belgrade in the 90s, and not by accident. The weed was strong, and Babylon was very real indeed. Another of the most popular protest groups, Kanda Kodza i Nebojsa, used reggae more explicitly. Eschewing Darkwood Dub's more elliptical style, they framed the spirit of resistance in direct language, singing of the *'final call'* which would be answered by the *'righteous ones'*. It was Peter Tosh reinterpreted for the Balkans. *'Their time will pass'* one of their songs urged. Heard out of context, their agit-dub groove wasn't life-changing. It didn't seem to matter. As a catalyst, it was working.

Musical epiphanies tend to be purely sonic — hearing 'White Riot' or 'Public Enemy No 1' tearing out of the radio for the first time, or Derrick May and Adonis shaking the sound system in the heady darkness of a club — and are often private moments, or shared among small groups of likeminded friends. But in Belgrade in 1996, as the city went critical, music had a communal resonance that went beyond its own world. It wasn't just an insurrectionary noise, it mirrored and amplified the prevailing mood of desperate urgency, becoming an integral part of a wider social move-ment that appeared, in the moment, as if it could actually prevail. Fela Kuti once said that music was a weapon, a call sign for revolution. Here it was... in full effect.

At the centre of it all was the courageous independent radio station B92, a beacon for musical progressives in Belgrade with its imaginative programming policy, but also one of the few news media outlets that was telling the truth about what was going on in the country. It had begun as a student broadcaster, and throughout the war years had tried to keep alive the idea that another kind of life in Serbia — cultural as well as political — was possible. Tens of thousands of disillusioned young people emigrated from Serbia during the 90s; B92 was the voice of those who stayed and tried to fight back. When the protests of 1996 began, it helped channel the energies that were coursing through the city — something the authorities weren't unaware of. Its signal was repeatedly jammed, then cut off entirely, not for the first time and not for the last. But it was soon back on air.

Looking down from B92's towerblock studio as the DJ played Curtis Mayfield's 'Move On Up' and St Etienne's 'Nothing Can Stop Us' and a quarter of a million demonstrators converged on the city centre, chanting down Milosevic with noisy fervour, it seemed that this was an irresistible force that would sweep like a breaking wave over the capital, washing away the hated government. But it wasn't to be. The wave ultimately broke and receded — Milosevic remained in power. It would take almost four more years for the resistance to gather the strength again to finish the job.

Matthew Collin is an editor at the Balkan Investigative Reporting Network

It was an exciting day when the first turntable arrived in the
Wire office. Up until then we'd had to rely on some poncy
old cassette player if we wanted to hear any music. Before
that, records had to sit patiently in their sleeves before any
audition, as records do. They stand there in rows, waiting for
eager fingers to riffle through them, the neverending browse
that only reaches a temporary hiatus when — for no reason
that I've ever quite figured out — the synapses induce a halt
and the mind settles on that particular one for the stylus to
rumble over.

Sometimes I think my whole life has been measured
out in piles of records: 45 years of riffling through. Sade
once told me that she couldn't imagine going through life
without a big record collection, and I think that was about
the only time I felt any empathy with her. Records have
driven everything. I don't just mean vinyl, either: 45s and 33s
(we used to call them that) were comparative latecomers for
me. One Christmas, my father put some remaindered Top
Rank 45s in my stocking, and I became acquainted with an
oddball assortment of groups including Harry Douglas & The
Deep River Boys, Larry Kirby & The Encores and The Wise
Guys (their 'Big Noise' is surely a forgotten masterwork).
But before that, I'd become fascinated by shellac, or 78s. One
day, when I was about five or six, a family friend brought
round a box of sleeveless 78s which he'd ferretted out from
somewhere and my parents produced a portable windup
gramophone from the boxroom in our house. From that day
on, I began collecting records, haunting local jumble sales
and fetes.

In the end, I went on to vinyl, because 78s — or at least,
any that interested me — were starting to become harder
to find, and I was getting involved in more modern music
anyway. But 78s started me out on jazz. It's all but impossible
for someone who starts with contemporary jazz to work
their way back to the beginning now: the greatest period

in jazz — 1923-25 — is so far away that you might as well be shaking hands with Beethoven as King Oliver. And those records sound dreadful to modern ears — acoustic recordings buried under decades of scratch.

Except they never sounded that way to me. If anything, I liked the surface noise of old records (which is probably the only empathy I have with Christian Marclay). These huge objects (remember I was pretty small when I started out), with their dark, shiny surfaces and inwardly spiralling groove, released sounds that could resemble a primeval roar. When you hear old records on a good gramophone, they don't sound 'better' in hi-fi terms, but they surely sound more immediate, the people embedded in the disc seeming to step out and greet you. It's only when you hear a cylinder play on an original phonograph that you understand why people called them 'talking machines': there seems to be a voice embodied in the reproducing horn itself. The surrounding hiss and crackle somehow seems like a necessary bandage, protecting the old ghost which the record is keeping safe.

Any collector will tell you about the thrill of approaching a pile of 78s, preferably still in musty original sleeves, at a junkshop or bootfair: you never know what buried treasure may be there, even though it's usually nothing. And when vinyl too began to become a widespread field of potential collecting conquest, I began to skulk around markets and secondhand shops looking for beat groups and jazz EPs. I shake my head now at the number of times I must have got up at dawn on a Sunday to get the first bus to Brick Lane in East london. It's all a bit gentrified there now, but you should have seen it in the 70s...

Somehow, even when I was an impoverished civil servant, I always had money for records. But the problem with a collecting jones is that you can never feed it enough. It seemed to me that music journalism, with its suggestion that you never had to pay for records again, was a good thing to look into. So it ultimately proved, although little did I suspect that by the time several editions of *The Penguin Guide To Jazz On CD* had gone past, I'd be buying and spending more than I ever had before. Or that packages of glistening new LPs would actually be a matter of the past, and instead it would be hefty jiffy bags, stout with jewel-cased compact discs.

I know — people always say you can't get excited about CDs, not the way you could with LPs. And like any other collector, I see that point of view — the hearty thickness of prime cardboard sleeves, especially the 60s flip-backed variety, is as cherishable in its way as the stately beauty of plum-label HMV 78s. But I want to be enlightened about this: I'm into it for the music as well as the artefact appeal, and I like CDs. I don't want new music to sound as if it's coming off a 78, and like anyone else I enjoy the convenience. Besides, I've got 10,000 of the damn things, and they cover the walls of my workroom like the velvet lining of a coffin.

No, I'm not going to be buried with them. Once a collector's work is done in this world, it's done, and besides, there wouldn't be a mausoleum big enough. As I've got older, I like to think (although my wife won't agree) that I've got this habit under control. These days, I mostly wait for records to come to me, via auction lists or contacts: that's the privilege of getting old. I've taken to acquiring vocal records, lately, from the earliest years of the 20th century, what one of the first record collectors, PG Hurst, described as 'the pinnacle of the collector's ambition': the voices of such as Felia Litvinne, Anastasia Vialtzeva, Giovanni Zenatello. Records resplendent with their red or black G&T labels, the voices trumpeting out, survivals of almost 100 years of possible damage or destruction. There wasn't anything as good as those in that box someone gave me, four decades ago. I loved them all the same.

Richard Cook was a UK music critic, author, editor and broadcaster. He died in 2007 aged 50

CATHAL COUGHLAN ON THE WAR SONGS OF SLAPP HAPPY AND ART BEARS

Greater than the fear of death, I think, is the fear that the passage of time will first diminish us before erasing us altogether. Companions vanish, connections also, and the imagined milestones of our imagined progress are revealed as empty vanities.

This is the story of an epiphany which has gone on giving through 36 years of my life. In the summer of 1975, while spending a sulky teenage holiday on my aunt's farm, at the the top of a hill in West Cork, I tuned in one night to Ireland's one full-time radio station of that time, to a show whose Irish language title and presentation entitled it to play a bafflingly wide range of modern music. This was anything but typical of the station.

I heard something which startled me that night. It was called 'War'.

It began with looping piano and drums, lurching over-excitedly, over which a faintly louche male American voice exhorted, *'Tell of the birth, tell how war appeared on earth'*, to be answered by a Central European female, rolling her Rs chidingly as she chanted, *'Thunder and herbs, conjugated sacred verbs, musicians with gongs, fertilised an egg with song'*.

The woman's delivery grew rapidly more venomous, and then the whole thing dissolved into gales of rhythmic, mirthless choral laughter. Then back to the top of the slope, to lurch down again. Eventually, there was a disorderly but tonal trumpet solo, and piano vamping which sounded like 'Virginia Plain' by way of Penderecki's back garden.

It seemed to be over in an instant (two and half minutes, in our Earth time). It laid waste to my perception of popular music as surely as its subject matter had done to Europe prior to that flared decade in which I sulked, with its flimsy escapism and auguries of conflict merely suspended.
The announcer told us that it was the work of 'Henry Cow agus Slapp Happy'. I was changed by it, but not then equipped for it.

In a slightly more urban setting, in 1981, here was an Art Bears album for £1.49. I saw that it was mainly the work of three of the people who created 'War', and in particular its female vocalist, Dagmar Krause. I hadn't read about it in any music papers, but the price was right, and it wasn't 'rockist', I didn't suppose...

The album began with voice, bassoon and violins, which not a lot of current music did at that time; the elements created an icy stillness in which dread was the only solid element. *'In such a country, and at such a time, there should be no melancholy evenings'*. These were Bertolt Brecht's words, 'On Suicide', originally composed in the 1920s, later set to music by Hanns Eisler.

Dagmar would later go on to record two classic albums of Brecht settings, her ever elastic and enthralling voice showcased against more expansive arrangements, but just as much as those, this very spare Art Bears recording is one to which I often return, and cannot be without. In the years of peripatetic living which followed, though, only a cassette recording of this one track from its kaleidoscopic parent album, *Hopes And Fears*, would accompany me on my circuitous pilgrimage to the heart of the gibberish that was most pop music in the 1980s.

In Camden High Street in North London in 1984, I was seeking to cope with the after-effects of a bad acid trip I'd had the night before, carrying the proofs for the artwork of my band's long delayed first album. From a record shop's stereo came a sound which hit my frazzled brain full force — a spectral, concrete-textured thing with murmured lyrics describing a dead-of-night incursion into the narrator's house by a group of strangers who ignore him and molest his female bedmate. The familiarity of the singer's voice nagged at me.

It turned out to be the album *The Naked Shakespeare* by Peter Blegvad, the American voice, and the lyricist, of 1975's 'War'. Rather like a non-harrowing *Music For A New Society*, its time of birth detectable, but not kitsch or dated, it defined an intersection of relatively conventional melodies with arcane and unpredictable predilections, which surface in the lyrics and in the songs' delivery. The words eschewed simple exhortation, but this record buoyed me up for a long time.

The latest instance of this intermittent epiphany happened in 2007, when I was working as a singer in musical theatre in Brittany. My now dying custom of seeking out unheard music on physical objects when travelling brought me into contact with the album *Songs*, by John Greaves, the bassist on 'War'.

Focusing on the 'art song' aspect of many phases of Greaves's work as a songwriter, and mainly featuring vocalists other than himself, including spectacular appearances by Robert Wyatt ('The Song') and Susan Belling ('Swelling Valley'), its style reflects his long residency in France, being by turns romantic and anarchic. A tune which begins as a fairly straightforward piano ballad will smoothly metamorphose into free blowing, then into a vocal mantra in an indecipherable time signature. And it works. 2008's *Verlaine* is even better.

I have no idea whether any of my own work approaches the heights achieved by Krause, Blegvad, Greaves, or by any of the similarly prolific and storied cocreators of that recording of 'War', and I don't intend to ever tax my spirits by seeking to reach a considered view on it.

But I'm grateful that I had the good fortune to live part of my life in a time when the association of pieces of music with known individuals and groups, while toxic in so many other ways, has allowed me to have an idea as to what a substantial body of work created by a non-celebrity might look like. What my own might look like, had I the inspiration and persistence to pursue it over the necessary lifelong period — it's not immortality, but I imagine it to be the echo of that.

Cathal Coughlan is an Irish singer and songwriter

JERRY DAMMERS ON HIS APPRECIATION OF SUN RA AND HIS COSMIC MUSIC

Although I am no jazz musician, I have loved jazz since the 1960s and have been aware of Sun Ra as long as I can remember. I saw him with The Arkestra at the Venue in London in the early 1980s, around the time of his song 'Nuclear War', when The Arkestra was still very large, and that was one of the best gigs I've ever seen. I think the epiphany, though, came sometime in the early 1990s. My hopeless search for breakbeats led me to Sun Ra's *Lanquidity* album from 1978. I was giving up smoking dope at the time and finding it a bit hard going. I guess I was looking for an alternative form of mental relaxation. By the time I'd got to the last track on *Lanquidity*, I was quite 'gone', as the saying goes, and I suddenly realised it was just the music, no ganja! Sun Ra was always dead against drugs, but went places most dope addled musicians never dreamt of, so in one go he had (a) relaxed my throbbing brain, (b) destroyed the myth that making truly 'out there' music has anything to do with drugs, and (c) destroyed the other myth that it has anything to do with being young (he must have been about 60 when he made *Lanquidity*). A woman's voice was scarily whispering, *'There are other worlds they have not told you of'* (the title of the last track), and it all seemed to somehow add up to some sort of positive way forward (way out?).

I formed a band called Jazz Odyssey (after the song in *This Is Spinal Tap*) and we played some funky Sun Ra-influenced type music including a Sun Ra cover. We sneaked into Glastonbury pretending to be another band, and held a free pop festival inside, but sadly it was to be our only gig. My dream of a genuine Sun Ra tribute band was not realised until 2006 when I formed The Cosmic Engineers, to play at the newly reopened Roundhouse in North London as part of Arts Catalyst's Space Soon week. The band has since been renamed The Spatial AKA Orchestra (aka The Spatials?).

So how did I get from ska to Ra? It's not such a huge leap. The best instrumental ska is basically 'away' spiritual jazz over a street rhythm, which is a similar idea to what we try to do in the orchestra. We do a Coxsone Dodd Japanese ska tune, blended with a Ra tune. Anyway, The Specials might have been a sort of ska band, but it was also a sort of cutting edge retro band too (mod postmanism?).

Normally I prefer tribute bands to the real thing, but in this case (the orchestra) we know that would be impossible because the real thing (Sun Ra's Arkestra) was basically the most perfect and coolest band ever, possibly because Ra had the best manifesto for a band ever. He had supposedly been abducted by aliens and sent back to Earth to teach us humans about the music of Saturn. This did make criticism a bit difficult, it has to be said. Ra was the master of the (black?) art of jive talk, which was political in itself — the 'lie' that tells the higher truth (about the position of black people in America). (If you're an alien reading this, and you abducted him, sorry.)

Across the majority of his phenomenal output (of at least 150 albums), he did manage to make his manifesto seem almost believable (which was the whole point, he set an almost impossible creative task for himself). You can find a passage of most modern sounds somewhere in Ra's output, seemingly light years before anybody else did it. For example, there is a track called 'Call For All Demons' recorded in 1956, part of which sounds exactly like The JBs, 15 years ahead of them. Like ska musicians, Ra was heavily influenced by exotica such as Les Baxter and Martin Denny. His versions of Walt Disney tunes supposedly completely confused Stockhausen, who liked Ra's freeform stuff. It seems the aliens had instructed Ra correctly, and he was well ahead — those exotica artists have received a bit of recognition in avant garde circles in recent years. Sun Ra suffered the unusual fate of being perceived by the general public as being purely 'difficult' music, because his more 'accessible' funkier stuff was largely ignored (because the European avant garde didn't understand it at the time?).

Ra's credentials as a master jazz pianist were well established and he had also apparently studied classical music. Maybe some of his imagery evolved because he was actually one of the few jazz musicians who mixed jazz with

European electronic (originally classical) music, which it seems was only acceptable in America if it was described as space age music (possibly to tie in with the Cold War race to the moon: in competition with the Soviets, both sides having carved up the Nazi rocket technology and grabbed Nazi scientists). Sun Ra, on the other hand, seemed to be saying that black people may not have had the resources to physically go to the moon, but they could travel through space anyway (through music). His space imagery possibly helped avoid a few raised eyebrows in the orthodox jazz world, and in the black political atmosphere of the times too (for his fusions with European electronic music).

The *Lanquidity* album made me aware of Sun Ra's more funky, African, repetitive, hypnotic side, which I found out later had always been there, as I said, largely ignored by the avant garde. Maybe he had the last laugh, though, because, just as a lot of what was referred to as 'modern art' in Europe actually developed from Picasso being influenced by African masks, so African music had always been 'abstract' in the sense of more emphasis on percussive sounds as opposed to notes. Sun Ra came to believe in 'tones not notes' (a typically great Ra wordplay).

In the late 1980s and 90s, towards the end of his life, maybe the introduction of pseudo-flash digital keyboards caught him a bit off guard, like a few other jazz musicians. To my ears, the 'tones' of those keyboards weren't as thick and dark and mysterious, and for the first time in a lifelong career he was slightly out of sync. I have a load of broken old analogue keyboards in the orchestra, I'm sort of trying to get at the sounds of those instruments as much as the notes. Zoe Rahman (pianist) brings the quality, I bring the quantity.

I hope Sun Ra would know that what we try to do with his music is meant to be a heartfelt tribute: he has continued to represent the ultimate in a certain something for generations now, it's hard to pinpoint exactly what it is. To me, it's some sort of ultra-free funk jazz with electronica and exotica in the mix.

Jerry Dammers is a UK musician and former leader of The Specials

I'm not sure if it's all the time I used to spend in zendos, but
when I find myself in a modern American symphony hall, I
usually treat these highly coded and uptight environments as
an invitation to focused attention. Once everybody shuts up
and the music starts, I sit as still as possible, sans the usual
pint, and devote myself to listening, with mind and heart in
as much sync as I can muster. This attitude, which can often
be as worthwhile as the music itself, really comes in handy
when the pieces performed are not the usual warhorses,
but the sort of 'challenging' and unfamiliar modern and
contemporary works I can appreciate in recordings but often
find tough to engage with while I am writing or puttering
around the house.

And so it was that I settled with rapt passivity into
my orchestra seat for The San Francisco Symphony's first
performance of Ligeti's monstrous 1965 *Requiem*. After a
tasty Baroque bonbon conducted by the Symphony Chorus
director Ragnar Bohlin, Michael Tilson Thomas took the
tiller, offered a few words of gentle warning, quoted Rilke,
and dove into 25 minutes of supreme apocalyptic weirdness.

Said to be partly inspired by the composer's own
reactions to the Holocaust, during which his entire family
save his mother was killed, Ligeti's *Day Of Wrath* melts
historical horror into an underworld of universal and
sometimes impish dread. The ominous drift of the opening
'Introitus', with some Gyuto monk-worthy growling from
the basses, soon splintered like some shuddering ice crystal
planet into the mountainous chromatic clouds of the 'Kyrie'.
Twisted into skeins of galactic dust, the massed human
voices became a fractal dance of dissolution and dynamic
crystallisation, the perpetual solve et coagula of Ligeti's
justly celebrated micropolyphony. The fluctuating lines and
hair-splitting intervals that make up the music's 20 separate
contrapuntal parts transformed the hall with an organic
underworld of half congealed aethyrs, so tricksy and difficult

for the chorus to pull off that a number of singers sported tuning forks.

I am not the most intellectual or analytic listener. Whenever the opportunity affords itself, I go for transport. Give me a keening emotion, an exotic evocation, an entrancing drone, a psychedelic arabesque, and I am outta here. Within minutes, the disturbing immensity of Ligeti's soundworld lifted me out of my seat. As the usual Cartesian coordinates of melody, harmony and pitch became lost in a chromatic atmosphere at once iridescent and opaque, all familiar reference points — the concert hall, the singers, the city beyond — seemed to melt into a claustrophobic and towering soundscape against the frightening backdrop of Pascal's infinite spaces. Even the hair on the back of my neck came to attention, and I submitted to an ominous undertow of awe.

Somewhere during the 'Kyrie' this transport became epiphany, a far rarer occurrence in my lexicon of listening. Instead of acting as a drug or a dreamlike trance, the *Requiem* became a mirror of the act of listening itself. Music melted into sound, sound into an almost tactile polyverse of now now now. The hall became a stage where the self that witnesses the waveforms of musical material realises its own identity as a wave of vibration. My whole body became an ear, jolts of energy tickled my spine, and the rhetoric of apocalypse — which means, of course, revelation — bloomed into a stark and impersonal unveiling of music as such — not the abstraction of 'absolute music', but the luminous roar of organised sound as a fundamental dimension of reality. This got me so tripped out that, when the hotshot Argentine pianist Martha Argerich took on Ravel's G major piano concerto after the intermission, I could barely relate. The piece was sparkling, her playing was rich with confidence and wit, and the crowd was in love, far more than they had been with Ligeti. But the music sounded to me like a Wurlitzer organ cranking away in a carnival as the aftershocks of some stellar catastrophe faded in the far atmosphere.

Reflecting on this experience later on, I realised that my epiphany could be boiled down to the simple Pavlovian fact that, like millions of earthlings, I first encountered Ligeti's eerie choral micropolyphony in the film *2001: A Space Odyssey*. A passage of Ligeti's 'Kyrie' is associated with the inky black monolith whose appearance heralds and may actually trigger breakthroughs in human consciousness. Coupled with Kubrick's images of chilly sublimity, Ligeti's sounds become another sort of extraterrestrial artefact, a literally otherworldly chorus composed equally of angels and aliens. Ligeti, of course, did not especially care for this exposure, and he also spent six years trying to prise some compensation out of MGM for their unauthorised use of his music. Nonetheless, Kubrick's appropriation can only be seen as a kindness of mutual infection. The film not only exposed millions of people to real-deal experimental music — in effect squeezing pop exoticism out of a product of the intellectual elite — but also trained the minds of moviegoers like me to map the more obvious imaginative transports of visual media onto the incorporeal vectors of intensely novel music.

A pop fusion of 'cosmic' sounds and images all too often becomes a kind of kitsch, from New Age poofery to space age bachelor pad soundtracks to the comic book pulp of 1970s prog. But this cartoon excess should not obscure the subtler ways in which Ligeti's *Requiem* engages the extraterrestrial imagination, and that can account, beyond the monolith association, for its enormous evocative power. Ligeti himself often used spatial metaphors to describe his work, almost as if we are forced to imagine the kind of parallel world capable of housing such music. We are impelled by imaginative necessity to speak of masses, crystals, tapestries, fractals. Discussing the way his rigorous contrapuntal structure is submerged inaudibly in his music, Ligeti himself spoke of the 'very densely woven cobweb' of his choral writing. In the manner of the imagination, this image triggers another — a childhood dream in which Ligeti finds himself entangled in a giant web, along with various insects and decaying pieces of junk. In the dream, he became a captive witness to the gradual transformation of what Philip K Dick would recognise as the 'tomb world', as the insects struggled to free themselves from the perpetually shifting web, like human voices that wake us as we drown.

Erik Davis is a US author and journalist

The grunge era of the early 1990s was one of the best periods in my life. I was young and broke and living in Toronto, but despite paying for beers with lint-covered nickels and dimes, my friends and I were still able to have an active social life, alternating between going to concerts during the week and heading to clubs that played garage and house on weekends. I was recently reminiscing with my best friend about those times, and she didn't wax nostalgic as much as I did. She remembered the fights (including one bizarre hair-pulling incident), hanging out and getting drunk with some unsavoury men, and the fact that because clubs didn't see young and single black women as economically viable, we sometimes watched our white friends get in while we were turned away at the door.

We also remembered how difficult it could be at testosterone-filled grunge concerts. We were usually the only black women in the room, and the men, not knowing what to do with us, either sneered or ignored us, sometimes physically shoving us aside. There was this underlying feeling that, because we didn't fit into the common stereotypes about black women — we weren't there to accompany our boyfriends but to get in the pit — we were undesired. Eventually my best friend opted out of going to shows with me, and I went looking for another black woman who I could commiserate with in this aggressive music scene.

I grew up in an era that was heavily influenced by music videos on heavy rotation on Canada's only music video station, MuchMusic. It seemed natural to be into Soundgarden, Pearl Jam, Screaming Trees and even some of the heavier non-grunge groups like Monster Magnet, White Zombie, Pantera and The Rollins Band. I had moved to Toronto in 1988 to attend college but it wasn't until the early 1990s that I was able to afford cable. As soon as I was hooked up, I spent hours watching MuchMusic, alternating between their regular programming and their genre-specific shows, such as *Soul In The City*. VJ Michael Williams was an

American transplant from Cleveland who, after first landing in Montreal, moved to Toronto and injected some soul into the lily-white metropolis. Programming videos and dropping some much needed background info on these relatively obscure black artists, whose music ranged from soul to funk to rock, Williams changed my life when he played The Family Stand's 'Ghetto Heaven'.

The house remix of the song eventually gained more popularity than the original, which was pure rock-funk at its finest. This version stood out for me, as it was the first time I had ever seen a contemporary black female rock artist. Not only was Sandra St Victor using her gospel-tinged soulful coo to accompany what was essentially a funked-up hard rock song, she was incredibly sexy and, more importantly, self-assured. I immediately fell in love with her confidence, and almost cried at the sight of this woman who represented a blend of a black-centric music sensibility with the aggressive sound that I loved. More important was how the infusion of black-centric music with a classic rock sound sounded like the best of both worlds. Later on the show Williams played 'Cry Baby' by Mother's Finest, a rock ballad that, while very 1980s in its sound, was another example of how 'black rock group' didn't just mean that the members were 'black' and doing 'white' music, but how they accentuated it to make their own unique blend.

As I started working as a music journalist, I unearthed several other black rock outfits that, based on Canada's limited exposure, felt like revelations: The Ike And Tina Turner Revue, Betty Davis, Parliament-Funkadelic, Bad Brains, and newer groups such as Living Color, Fishbone and Weapon Of Choice, whose fiery lyrics perfectly suited my political views. These groups made me feel better about my schizophrenic life: a black militant and social justice activist immersed in white music. The music's aggression suited the inner frustration I was experiencing but was encouraged not to openly express. But the contemporary groups primarily consisted of men, who, as I learned much later, were less likely to generate consternation in others because of their music preferences.

Sometime between 1994 and 1995, my heart skipped a beat again when I saw the video of Skunk Anansie's 'Selling Jesus'. The sight of a group fronted by a tall, shaven-headed black woman called Skin yelling from my TV screen was mesmerizing. The music was heavier and punkier than The Family Stand and Mother's Finest, and was more to my liking. That was it. This is who I want to be. I quickly got dressed and headed to the local record store to look for Skunk Anansie's debut album *Paranoid & Sunburnt*, only to have a bit of trouble finding it. With Skin prominently featured on the album cover, the store had categorised it as R&B. I had been looking in the hard rock section.

This actually served as a premonition because, in hindsight, it was the moment I discovered how difficult it was for black women to be seen to be performing aggressive music. While researching *What Are You Doing Here? A Black Woman's Life And Liberation In Heavy Metal*, I was able to interview the women who had served as my idols and inspiration for discussing black women musicians and fans in these scenes: Sandra St Victor and Skin. They discussed their struggles, but even more so their victories as black women vocalists, and how important it was to make yourself known, even in places where we aren't expected to be.

Laina Dawes is a Canadian music journalist and author

My dad was an organic chemistry professor, an eccentric
sort who would often reel off Sanskrit quotes and organic
chemistry formulae in the same stream of consciousness
sentence. He spent lots of time reading in his office in the
cellar, with teetering piles of dusty chemistry texts stacked in
every conceivable corner. A single photo of Einstein adorned
the bare white wall. When I asked my dad why he admired
him, he glossed over the physics and said it was because
Einstein cycled to work and refused to comb his hair.

When my dad wasn't thinking about weird science, he
thought about weird music. I was a science obsessive and a
music obsessive, too. The problem was, our tastes in music
diverged wildly and often. My favourite music as a little kid
was pop. Meanwhile, he was immersed in Indian classical
music by the likes of Zakir Hussain and Ravi Shankar. My
dad was a fairly accomplished tabla and harmonium player,
and I'd often wake up on weekends to the sounds of him
playing ragas in the living room as the sun rose. He was eager
to share his enthusiasm for his music, but my eyes glazed
over the minute I heard it. Sometimes he would take me to
Indian classical concerts and I'd fall fast asleep, what with the
constant repetition, lengthy soloing, the insistent soothing
drone of the tanpura...

Year: 1987. I'm eight years old and we're on the annual
holiday to a cottage on a lake in New Hampshire. I take out
the cassette tape in the car — one of my dad's beloved Indian
classical music tapes — and put in my very first cassette
purchase: *The White Album*.

'Turn this rubbish off!' ordered my dad.

'But dad, it's The Beatles! They were popular when you
were young!'

'I don't care who 'The Beatles' are. Turn it off!'

My dad couldn't stand The Beatles, or most other
Western rock and pop music for that matter. To this day, he
doesn't know David Bowie, or The Stones, or any of that lot.

Maybe it didn't make sense — more likely, it just bored him. He shook his head when he saw me watching MTV. To him, it was all horrible noise.

The music he loved best had no melodies I understood. It favoured endless repetition over an attractive pop package. Verses bled into other verses with no discernible choruses. It all seemed formless to me at the time. I would fall asleep almost immediately just listening to it.

My mother only listened to Hindu religious music. The house was crammed full with her tapes. She had a temple room upstairs with marble Krishna deities that she'd bought in Jaipur, and often I'd find her sitting there with her eyes closed, listening to circular, repeating chants for hours on end. She'd go to marathon prayer sessions at the local Hindu temple that lasted all night, where groups would pray with the same call-and-response chants for hours.

I didn't understand my parents, or their culture. Unlike them, I'd been born and raised in America. What started out as boredom and irritation with Indian music as a child became a passionate rejection of Indian music — and all things Indian — as a snarling, rebellious teenager. I cut most of my black hair off and dyed the rest of it purple, then red, then blue, then green. I listened to punk rock and sported leather, steel-toed boots and a bad attitude. When I pierced my nose at age 18, though, my mother was pleased because she thought I was finally embracing my Indian heritage. But rebellion — and hair dye — fade, and soon after getting to university I got interested in, er, experimentation of different sorts.

Year: 1997. I went to MIT to study chemistry with the goal of being a chemistry professor, just like my dad. Somewhere along the way, I decided I never liked chemistry much and I'd rather be a writer. My dad was heartbroken. A few years later, after reluctantly finishing my science degree, I went back to his office in the cellar and flipped through his organic chemistry textbooks. Yellowed, tattered pages fell out of the books — poems by Wordsworth, Keats, Yeats. I asked him about them. 'I never much wanted to do chemistry when I was your age,' he admitted. 'I liked poetry. I wanted to be a writer.'

I felt I understood my dad better then, but what made me understand him more was my growing interest in more exploratory music, from obscure techno to krautrock to field recordings to the wilder reaches of jazz. I took courses in music composition. A class in Western counterpoint and harmony was easy enough, but a class in Indian music composition was intensely difficult. I started to see how Indian classical music was crawling with infinitely complex patterns, and how it trained you to listen to sounds differently. And it was then that I realised that my dad just heard music in a different way — he found beauty in endless repetition, discerned shape in sounds that seemed shapeless. And I found that my reluctant exposure to his music when I was small informed me, in some way, in whatever I listened to now. My love for Neu! can be traced back to Indian music and the ecstatic feeling that comes from constantly looping chants. My love for The Fall stems, at least partially, from my tolerance for repetition. My mother's all-night temple blissouts helped me to understand rave culture and dance music. I became interested in minimalism, and the more I read about its formal ties to Indian music, the more it made sense. Instead of The Beatles, I played different stuff for my dad in the car: Terry Riley, microhouse, Sun City Girls. He was into it, and suddenly I realised how hip my dad always was.

Year: 2004. It's a hazy Saturday evening in New York, and I'm in my hideout from the city grind — La Monte Young's Dream House on Church Street. I lie down on the white carpet, my head perched on a white pillow, absorbing drones through every fibre of my body. There's a little shrine to Pandit Pran Nath in the corner, with some candles and incense. I started to think that maybe I should take my parents here sometime — they'd probably like this place. They were the ones who taught me to like this music, after all.

Geeta Dayal is a US journalist and author

BRIAN DILLON ON THE FEELINGS UNLEASHED BY
KATE BUSH'S *HOUNDS OF LOVE*

In the summer of 1985 my mother died. I had just turned
16. My parents had known for weeks that the auto-immune
disease that pinched and harrowed my mother's flesh for
years had finally turned on her major organs, and there was
no hope. My two younger brothers and I were not informed.
But we knew that things had altered for the worse — there
must have been a reason that my father kept us from the
hospital this time. Meanwhile, relatives gathered and
maintained a quiet version of normality. On Saturday 13
July my brothers and I sat dazed in front of the spectacle of
Live Aid. My father came back late and went to bed, but we
carried on watching into the night.

 Four days later the hospital phoned and we were rushed
to our mother's bedside. She died shortly before noon. Of the
weeks that followed, I remember mostly silence. My father,
a reticent man destroyed by grief, spoke of my mother once
('Pray for her'), and never again. We took his lead — I didn't
talk to my brothers about her for 20 years. Instead we had
music, the sole currency by which we expressed what had
happened to us. And even music, in the aftermath, seemed
too much for our mute household to bear. It was October
when I dared to buy a record: the second single from an album
released in the autumn as I went back to school and faced the
public shame of being semi-orphaned. 'Running Up That Hill'
had been the first hint: a darkling ecstasy erupting in the dog
days on teatime television. But it was 'Cloudbusting' — in the
aerated, insistent mix that accompanied its video — which
finally opened a wound of sorts in the atmosphere at home.
The single itself, when I played it in our sitting room with my
father unspeaking behind his newspaper, seemed brisker and
more tightly structured, but no less scandalous: a preternatu-
ral hymn to hope and loss. Though it was not true, it seemed
that Kate Bush's was the first female voice that sounded in our
house since my mother died. Playing the song to my father, I
dimly knew, was at once an act of spite and desperation.

The album, *Hounds Of Love*, came later. The cassette was a gift from a friend at school. We were not the closest of friends. He was a guitarist in a group I would shortly be thrown out of for total lack of musical ability and extreme pretension; our friendship consisted mostly of rancorous debates regarding the relative merits of our musical heroes, and things had lately reached an impasse when I pitched The Jesus And Mary Chain against his love of all things touched by the hand of Mark Knopfler. I wonder now about this tentative brotherhood of suburban Dublin boys, making ribald jokes about Kate and her dogs on the cover of *Hounds Of Love*, yet wholly seduced by the rigorous exhilaration of that album's first side. We were sure that something vastly strange and technically unprecedented had happened to this artist we remembered as an oddity, even an embarrassment. (We were wrong about that, of course, and not quite right that she was suddenly sexier than recalled.) But mostly, because (unsurprisingly) we never spoke about it, I wonder if my friend had paid much attention to 'Mother Stands For Comfort'.

For a year or so, *Hounds Of Love* was the secret medium in which I processed my mother's death. That is putting it too crudely: it's not that the record got me 'through' anything, if only because there was much else in the way of reckoning to come. Rather, the album was an education in various ecstasies I was too crushed to admit, as much a promise of love as of loss, quaking fear as riotous invention. The metaphoric scope of 'The Ninth Wave' song cycle, which occupies the album's second side, is well known: it's a record in thrall to images of capture and release, judgment and guilt, petrified feeling and ice shattering desire. But far more convulsing was its texture: those moments of delicate yearning suddenly accelerated into expansive apprehension of bodily and cosmic being. And all of this was deeply instructive as well as embarrassing — listening to *Hounds Of Love* was a compulsively shaming pleasure.

I knew at the time that there was another language for this record. It was the album on which Bush parlayed her kooky folk-hippy (but completely mainstream, children's television) persona into something approaching the apotheosis of

post-punk. If the record, sonically speaking, matched the best
of what was possible with the machined palette of mid-1980s
pop, it also sat uncannily easily alongside Foetus's *Hole*
and mid-period Cabaret Voltaire. If such company sounds
unlikely, consider the singer's stated admiration for Public
Image Limited — the writer Michael Bracewell has spoken of
hearing 'Running Up That Hill' for the first time and being
convinced it was the best record since PiL's (mother-haunted)
Metal Box. Bush seems to have briefly embraced her status
as faintly malevolent avant gardist: in 1986 she appeared on
TV flanked by massed Fairlights and lab-coated operatives
to perform the dystopian 'Experiment IV'. All of this is true,
and all of it inadequate to this particular epiphany — because
Hounds Of Love is also the record that taught me what feelings
might feel like when I finally got round to having them.

Brian Dillon is the UK editor of *Cabinet* magazine and a Reader in
Critical Writing at London's Royal College of Art

MICHEL FABER ON A SPONTANEOUS MUSIC
ENSEMBLE ENCOUNTERED IN THE BACK STREETS
OF BUDAPEST

It was dusk in Szentendre, a small town about 20km north
of Budapest, in 1991. I was in Europe for the first time since
emigrating from it as a child. My wife and I were being guided
by our new friend Janos, a Hungarian-American who took
our request to be spared the usual tourist sights very seriously.
It was winter and we had no way of knowing that in summer
the cobbled streets of this town are overrun with souvenir-
hunting foreigners. For us, Szentendre was spookily deserted.
The lamplit cobbles, glistening with recent rain, and the
immaculately preserved 18th century Balkan architecture,
wreathed in fog, seemed to embody all the ancient mystery
that sun-bathed Melbourne lacked.

We had no particular objective other than to wander,
but suddenly we were overtaken by a bunch of young men
running along the street carrying instrument cases — violin,
cello, trumpet, flute, I can't remember what else. 'We're
playing a concert, want to come?' they called in Hungarian
over their shoulders.

We followed them into a low-ceilinged cellar where
a few dozen people — mainly friends and family, I got the
impression — were seated, chatting quietly like patrons at
a classical concert. There was no alcohol on offer. Earnest
Slavic lads dressed in natty casuals and knitted sweaters
were adjusting cello stands and sheet music. A kitchen chair
was placed in front of an upright piano. An amateur recital,
it seemed.

The band was called After Crying. They had just made
their first LP, *Overground Music* (vinyl only, small stack of
copies available on a table upstairs). Janos bought one, and
later found it to be a poorly produced, awkward effort, an
exercise in what the band must have imagined might be
commercially viable in the big wide English-speaking world.
In the Szentendre cellar, however, After Crying did not
compromise.

What was it like? Progressive rock of the most unfashion-able kind — even more unfashionable in 1991 than it is today. It was sublime. A seamless interflow of nimble improvisation and elegant composition. Not a single cheap gesture, no ego displays, just profound concentration, gentle humour and genuine grandeur. I don't know if After Crying were aware of how contemptible any trendy Westerner would have considered them. My experience of pre-EU European coun-tries suggests not. One thing was for sure: the band performed with unashamed sincerity. At one point, Peter Pejtsik, the cellist, made an announcement about his cherished musical forebears. Janos murmured to us: 'He says, 'We're very influenced by King Crimson'.' Then, after a moment's hesitation: 'Or, to translate literally, 'We've suckled at the breast of Robert Fripp'.' Sure enough, when the band resumed their performance, I was delighted to hear some themes from *Lizard* (a little appreciated meisterwerk even among the most rabid Crimsoids) being quoted as part of the exquisite interplay between Pejtsik and pianist Csaba Vedres.

Now, I've been to some good gigs, gigs to talk about forever afterwards, gigs virtually guaranteed to impress anyone who wasn't there. The Birthday Party, Faust, Nico, the nascent Spiritualized in a tiny club in Newcastle, The Residents with Snakefinger in an Australian seaside pub, etc, etc. But After Crying were the best. And what's interesting to me all these years later, long after my specific memory of the music played that night has faded (or been stealthily supplanted by the roughly contemporaneous recordings available on the excellent two CD retrospective *Elsö Évtized*), is the challenge of convincing anyone how good it was.

The desire to be considered cool is a curse, especially among lovers of avant garde music who worry about their post-industrial halo being tarnished by baroque naffness. There is no cred to be gained enthusing about a Hungarian prog rock group, whereas if I told you how the crush at the Birthday Party gig pushed me forward onto the stage, so that I was squatting under Tracey Pew's crotch while an incensed Rowland Howard kicked a supine Nick Cave, yelling, 'Get up, ya cunt!'... Ah, I can see some people's eyes glaze over with envy already. To have been so near the epicentre of an explosion of Cool!

The inconvenient truth is that The Birthday Party were, on some level, merely going through the motions. They were trying so hard to be The Birthday Party. Same with Nico. Even at the time, in ignorance of the fact that she would soon be dead and untouchably 'great', I couldn't help feeling that her concert was less than fully authentic; Nico was not really free to make music. She was assuming the persona — 'legendary ex-Velvets chanteuse' — that she judged the punters had come to see. After Crying weren't concerned with their legend or leather boots. They were playing music that they loved, and cherishing every second of the opportunity to improvise with their friends.

After the finale, the musicians hung around, chatting to the audience, tinkering with their instruments some more. It was over and yet it wasn't over; they couldn't quite let go. Flautist Gabor Egervári had put down his piccolo but was attracted by the now unattended piano; he walked over to it and started caressing the keys, lost in thought. His little daughter, just tall enough to reach the keyboard standing, joined him. They improvised together, she plinking out some naive notes, he elaborating on them with tender sophistication. It was one of the loveliest things I've ever seen or heard. I thought to myself: This is real. This is happening right now, right here, and it will not happen again. No one outside this room will ever care about it. It will never attain mythic status. It will never be written about in *Q* or *The Wire*. And this is the fate of 99.99 per cent of all the marvellous music that has ever been made and that ever will be made. And it's OK.

Michel Faber is a Dutch born author

The 1970 Isle of Wight Festival has had a lot of ink. It took me many years to appreciate some of the great performances I heard there and just as long to understand the disappointment that I felt at the time, watching my heroes like Sly Stone come a cropper.

One great and wholly unanticipated triumph that is never spoken about was the explosive midnight contribution of The Voices Of East Harlem. The deep imprint of that tantalising encounter drew me, some six weeks later, to London's Royal Albert Hall for a chance to be reacquainted with them.

The young choir, some 15 or 16 voices strong, was bolstered artfully by a particularly energetic and skilful touring band. Their dazzling guitarist was Elliott Randall, shortly to find fame and fortune with Steely Dan thanks to his epoch-making contribution to 'Reelin' In The Years'. The bass player, Doug Rauch, was a cool, rangy androgyne in snakeskin boots who would go on to become a mainstay of Santana in their funkiest (*Caravanserai*) incarnation. I did not catch the names of the organist and the drummer, but today I can recall the glorious damage they did as if it happened last night.

The sound of massed, youthful voices marshalled by Bernice Cole had been enrapturing even in the bleak sonic environment of the festival. The Albert Hall was not known for its good acoustics but, lodged in the orchestra seats at the back of the stage on the right hand side, we picked up the breathy gale of sound being blown backwards from the onstage monitors. I sat with my schoolfriends just a few feet away from the performers, and being behind them cemented the illusion of our participation in their performance — a common pleasure of sitting in that cheap location.

I have no recollection of how full the hall actually was but the sound the group generated made it appear packed. The Voices started at high speed and tore through a selection of the effervescent material which would comprise their first Elektra album, *Right On Be Free*. Corny pop staples like 'Proud Mary' and 'Simple Song Of Freedom' were made over as R&B epics in which antiphony became not so much a musical technique as a cultural principle. Those tunes were intercut with adapted gospel standards like 'Music In The Air' and 'No, No, No', as well as Richie Havens's not-yet-classic 'Run Shaker Life', which was familiar from his Hyde Park gig supporting Blind Faith and his appearance at the Isle of Wight a year earlier. He seemed to be always in England then.

To my 14 year old ears, operating on funk frequencies conditioned almost exclusively by the benchmarks set by Sly and The Meters, The Voices' extended version of Buffalo Springfield's 'For What It's Worth' was the most outrageously syncopated second-line mutation I had encountered. Its storm of ludic, funny, excessive, generous, competitive, real-time, rhythmic play was something that I recognised without having adequate words to name. It fulfilled and compounded a need in me that 41 years later, I am no closer to being able to articulate. Even in the album's muddy, anodyne version it still makes me smile.

I had recently read Claude Brown's classic autobiography, *Manchild In The Promised Land*, so the very sound of the word Harlem was terrifying to me. However respectable they were in fact, this denim-clad, Afro-toting tribe of young Americans with their Donny Hathaway caps, Panther moves and Young Lords swagger, seemed to be the stylistic cutting edge of the dangerous contemporary world. We were poised on the edge of revolution and The Voices' profane appropriation of Stephen Stills confirmed the inevitability of countercultural triumph. We had bumped into one of them, a couple of years our junior, in the toilet just before the performance started and were paralysed with shyness even before we discovered that he was Kevin Griffin, who sang the lead on the Havens composition.

The period between the Isle of Wight show and the Albert Hall concert had been punctuated, midway, by the death of Jimi Hendrix. His name was not mentioned that night but he was, I think, in all our minds as The Voices' performance began to take on the quality of a grieving ritual for him. I recall in particular how wave after rolling wave of their exhilarating yet mournful music elevated the song 'Right On Be Free' into an anthemic exploration of despair, loss, yearning and ultimate transcendence. Searing fragments of the 'negro spiritual' were mashed up into the rasping tone of Randall's humbuckered Stratocaster and the dopplered pulse of the organ's Leslie cabinet as the growling voice of Geri Griffin occupied the musical space that the others had cleared for her: *'I want to go where the grey goose goes… high flying bird, high flying bird, fly by me'*. As the performance reached its conclusion, The Voices summoned us to join them on the stage. We scrambled down to do so without hesitation, dancing together around the musicians and, in a precious moment of impossible, Ellisonian bliss, we fell irrecoverably into the music itself.

The Voices never produced a record which captured the power of their early live shows. Perhaps that would not have been possible. I'm sure the constraints of touring on that extravagant scale would have circumscribed their musical and commercial options. A few years later, they were briefly beneficiaries of London's rare groove vogue through their 'Can You Feel It' collaboration with Leroy Hutson on *Just Sunshine*. I found that trophy record in a barbershop in Cleveland, Ohio.

I am still close to the dear friend with whom I shared that rare and delightful exposure to the elemental force of human imagination, even though the political aspirations that framed it on that extraordinary night faded long ago.

Paul Gilroy is a UK Professor of American and English Literature at London's King's College

MICHAEL GIRA ON THE SOUNDS OF FEAR AND LOATHING

In 1967 I was, if I may say so, a beautiful 13 year old California Boy with long blond hair and I lived in an idyllic beachside suburb of Los Angeles. When not in school — which I ditched regularly anyway — I was at the beach, at the local park where the freaks gathered, or along the Strand in Venice, where one might occasionally watch the Hell's Angels randomly pummel an errant hippy. I avidly consumed the music of The Doors, The Seeds, Love, Country Joe And The Fish (I can still hear 'Not So Sweet Martha Lorraine' — though I haven't listened to it since) and especially, The Mothers Of Invention. Frank Zappa was my idol. His snide rejection of all things plastic (Ha! Ha!), the freaked out weirdness of the music, and his gnarled appearance formed an attractive opposite to my sunny surroundings.

Unfortunately, I was also an enthusiastic consumer of another lure of hippy culture — drugs: Seconal, Nembutal, Benzedrine, Methedrine and, naturally, LSD. I studiously counted each dose of the latter and by 13 had tripped 200 times. I had a taste for anything chemical and mind churning — a rag dipped into the gas tank of a car served just as well as the inhaled fumes of Energine Spot Remover; with acid, this made for the ultimate in stupefaction. I had zero parental supervision. My mother, in whose care I resided, was a deeply committed alcoholic. She spent day and night sitting at her desk drinking in solitude — hallucinating and bitterly cursing with alarming eloquence the day my father (who'd absconded) was born. Drugs were bought with money stolen from her unguarded purse and by selling her jewels, cameras and our family collection of rare silver dollars. This couldn't go on forever. After several arrests for vandalism and general juvenile delinquency, I was expelled from my junior high school for smashing the plate glass window of the vice principal's office and was soon arrested again, this time stumbling and nearly comatose in a vacant lot with a baggy full of reds (Seconal capsules) dangling from my hand. That was it. The authorities set their ultimatum: either my father would come and get me or I would be taken from my mother and placed in a juvenile facility indefinitely.

He soon arrived, twisted my ear with military precision, and took me first to Indiana for a year (don't ask), and then to Paris, France, where he'd landed a job as a business consultant. It was 1969 now, and Paris was in the hedonistic afterglow of the student revolts. I did the right thing and promptly ran away. I survived for a time panhandling on the Pont Neuf, and was then taken under the wing of a group of feral Italian hippies. The leader had a mucus-encrusted beard, yellow curling fingernails, wore a mangy afghan coat, and carried a white rat on his shoulder. We all had lice. We ate leftover food from cafes, begged, drew inept chalk drawings on the sidewalk for tourists, and slept in abandoned buildings. After a few weeks word came of a huge music festival happening in Belgium. We split Paris and hitchhiked up to our psychedelic Mecca. We landed in cold mud, cow dung and straw, with thousands of other steaming and mouldy hippies. I was continuously and ravenously hungry, but somehow drugs never seemed to be a problem. They were everywhere. I have no idea what impression the music would have made without them.

The line-up included the following: Pink Floyd, The Art Ensemble Of Chicago, Anthony Braxton, Captain Beefheart, The Nice, Pretty Things, Archie Shepp, Soft Machine and my idol, Frank Zappa. This might sound like a muso's wet dream, but I confess I remember only a few key moments. The first is a SCREAM, courtesy of Pink Floyd. Sprawled in the dirt, I heard an amorphous, gathering tide of orchestral, but soothing sound. Then, suddenly everything erupted — cued by the scream — as if you'd been mindlessly drifting in warm water, hallucinating, and a lunatic beast is now attacking you with a butcher's knife, flinging shards of your body up to heaven. Wonderful! It's 'Careful With That Axe, Eugene', of course, though I didn't know it at the time. I doubt I'd ever even heard of Pink Floyd. All I know is it sent shockwaves of really, really bad vibes through my spine and the sensation was quite pleasurable indeed. It sprayed fountains of cleansing sulphuric acid on the filthy crowd. They needed it. I've never forgotten that moment (second?). It was the first instance I realised music could be more than a recitation and could actually alter you in a direct, experiential way. The only other time I've experienced a musical/sonic sensation that complete is with the music of Glenn Branca, much, much later. And, oh yes, Frank Zappa sat in with Pink Floyd on another song, and it truly, truly sucked. I lost interest in him forever right there. At that age, I had no reference or critical sensibility, but I hated guitar solos. This one intruded on the music in a stupid, ego-driven way, and he deflated before my eyes. Hilariously, the local troll-activists were waving banners while he played, calling him a capitalist for demanding money to perform — what did they expect?

But the most indelible moment was the rousing reception The Art Ensemble Of Chicago received. Imagine a steady rumble of what's now called skronk I guess — not loud, but persistent and undeniably intense, a ricochet of conflicting noises to most ears. I was gone, spinning on acid and had just smoked a massive arm-sized spliff, feeling the first deep tug of nausea as a result. But I was in it, right there with them, my fellow countrymen, just a blond haired kid from California down in the mud in a sea of ugly and increasingly scary troglodytes. Then, THE SOUND: a BIG low murmur, an endless exhalation of stinking gas. THE ENTIRE CROWD WAS BOOING — a sustained, deep drone of simian intolerance. They all chimed in, thousands of them — cows rising from a narcotic slumber, feeding each other's ugliness. It was and remains the most hideous and simultaneously mesmerising sound I've ever heard. I felt it reverberating in my belly (and reverberate it did: I threw up a psychedelic breakfast right there into my lap). I have measured everything I've done professionally against that amazing, unstoppable sound ever since. Ha! Ha! It was a warning, but I have to say, it also had a very seductive quality to it.

Michael Gira is a US musician, singer, songwriter and label runner

KENNETH GOLDSMITH ON THE JOY OF ACQUIRING MUSIC VIA
FILE SHARING NETWORKS

Epiphany No 1: While I could discuss any number of musical
epiphanies I've personally experienced over the past half a
century, all of them would pale in comparison to the epiphany
of seeing Napster for the first time. Although prior to Napster
I had been a member of several file sharing communities,
the sheer scope, variety and seeming endlessness of Napster
was mind-boggling: you never knew what you were going to
find and how much of it was going to be there. It was as if
every record store, fleamarket and charity shop in the world
had been connected by a searchable database and had flung
their doors open, begging you to walk away with as much as
you could carry for free. But it was even better, because the
supply never exhausted; the coolest record you've ever dug
up could now be shared with all your friends. Of course, this
has been exacerbated many times over with the advent of
torrents and MP3 blogs.

    Epiphany No 2: One of the first things that struck
me about Napster was how damn impure (read: eclectic)
people's tastes were. While browsing another user's files, I
was stunned to find John Cage MP3s alphabetically snuggled
up next to, say, Mariah Carey files in the same directory.
Everyone has guilty pleasures; however, never before had
they been so exposed — and celebrated — so publicly. While
such impure impulses have always existed in the avant
garde, they've pretty much remained hidden. For instance,
on UbuWeb we host a compilation of the ultra-modernist
conductor and musicologist Nicholas Slonimsky's early
recordings of Varèse, Ives and Ruggles. But we also host a
recording of Slonimsky croaking out bawdy tunes about
constipated children — *'Opens up the BOW-ELS'* — on an out
of tune piano. He sounds absolutely smashed. The Slonimsky
recording is part of The 365 Days Project, which is a collection
of crazy stuff: celebrity, children, demonstration, indigenous,
industrial, outsider, song-poem, spoken, ventriloquism, etc;
snuggled in with the crazy Mormons, twangy garage bands

and singing stewardesses is one of the fathers of the avant garde, Nicholas Slonimsky.

Epiphany No 3: File sharing is non-contextual. The cohesive vision of an album has been ditched in favour of the single or the playlist. Many people getting music online have no idea where something came from, nor do they care. For instance, we find that many people downloading MP3s from UbuWeb have no interest in the historical context; instead, the site is seen as a vast resource of 'cool' and 'weird' sounds to remix or throw into dance mixes. It has been reported that samples from Bruce Nauman's mantric chant, 'Get Out Of My Mind, Get Out Of This Room', from his *Raw Materials* compilation on Ubu, has recently been mixed with beats and is somewhat the rage with unwitting partygoers on dancefloors in São Paulo.

Epiphany No 4: As a result, just like you, I stopped buying music. I used to be a record junkie. For years, I spent most of my free time hunting down discs in dusty corners of the world. I'll never forget my honeymoon in Amsterdam in 1989. I had to purchase an extra suitcase so that I could bring home dozens of Dutch reissues of Stax and Atco soul LPs that were completely unavailable in New York. While I travel extensively these days, I haven't set foot in a record store in well over a decade. Why bother, when the best record store sits on my laptop in my hotel room? A few nights ago at home, after putting the kids to bed, I was parked in front of the computer sipping bourbon. My wife asked me what I was doing. I told her I was going record shopping. As I glanced at my screen, ten ultra-rare discs I would have killed for way back when were streaming down to my living room for free.

Epiphany No 5: I don't know about you, but I've lost my object fetish. But then again, I was never the type of collector who bought records for their cool covers: the music had to be great. Still, I have 10,000 vinyls gathering dust in my hallway and as many CDs in racks on my wall. I don't use them. To me, if music can't be shared, I'm not interested in it. However, once I digitize these objects and they enter into the file sharing ecosystem, they become alive for me again. As many dead LPs and CDs as I have, I've got many times that number of discs sitting on a dozen hard drives, flying up and down my network.

Epiphany No 6: It's all about quantity. Just like you, I'm drowning in my riches. I've got more music on my drives than I'll ever be able to listen to in the next ten lifetimes. As a matter of fact, records that I've been craving for years (such as the complete recordings of Jean Cocteau, which we just posted on Ubu) are languishing unlistened to. I'll never get to them either, because I'm more interested in the hunt than I am in the prey. The minute I get something, I just crave more. And so something has really changed — and I think this is the real epiphany: the ways in which culture is distributed have become profoundly more intriguing than the cultural artefact itself. What we've experienced is an inversion of consumption, one in which we've come to prefer the acts of acquisition over that which we are acquiring, the bottles over the wine.

Kenneth Goldsmith is a US poet, academic and writer and the founding editor of the online cultural archive UbuWeb

JONNY GREENWOOD ON THE IRRECONCILABLE
MUSICAL DIFFERENCES BETWEEN LIVE AND
RECORDED SOUND

In the mid-1990s, I went to an orchestral concert by the
Polish composer Krzysztof Penderecki. He was conducting
his *Viola Concerto* as part of some elaborate Polish arts event.
The venue was the Drapers' Hall in London — all white
and gold stucco, soft carpets. I felt very out of place: there
were Polish Embassy dignitaries everywhere, some wearing
medals, and not much English being spoken. It was all very
suited, very proper.

Then the concert started. I thought I knew what to expect,
because I was familiar with this stuff: I'd learnt, from scores
and recordings, that Penderecki's abstract music was all
about abrasion — fingernail/blackboard, horror films, painful,
simple noise. And I knew I could trust these recordings
because I was so proud of my hi-fi, with its carefully chosen
separate components, the well-reviewed speaker stands, the
optimum sitting position in the middle — we will examine this
shameful hi-fi snobbery later.

So, when the music began, when it started up from
silence in all this empty space, I was shown 30 magical,
confusing minutes that patiently demonstrated to me, over
and over, how wrong I was about everything. It changed how
I think of music, musical instruments, recordings, concerts —
I hope it put me right.

There was all this texture: quiet, delicate sounds, some
with a whispering complexity, others that hung in the air like
sparks. And what made it so beautiful was this convolution:
the strings as 48 separate sound sources, the space in the
room, the walls reflecting all these sounds, the effort of all
these players to make it happen. Too quiet to be abrasive, too
static to be just flurries of inconsequential notes, too dense to
make out the familiar sound of individual instruments — but
then, too complicated to just be 'noise'. It was fascinating and
beautiful, like watching a colony of ants making structures
with themselves, millions of moving bugs working together,

and presented right up close, every moving limb visible. I thought there must be speakers somewhere adding to the sound — it seemed impossible that these noises could come out of a few wooden instruments. When I write orchestral music now, I still think back to how it felt sitting in that room, and what was happening in the air around us.

Penderecki studied electronic music as a student in Warsaw, but then translated his knowledge of how those sounds were made — tone generators, filters, tape effects — into conventional orchestration, so that violins could reproduce these same colours. These so-called 'extended techniques' are now thought to be very dated. It's all very 60s — but then, I've sat in concert halls listening to hissy recordings of Moogs, and those sounds really have dated. I wonder if digital processing will have the same fate, with its granular processing, FFT treatments. To me, Penderecki's string orchestration still feels like a step forward, not back. It's all coming off paper. That feels modern to me too.

Compare the sound of white noise generated by an analogue synth to Penderecki's orchestral imitation of white noise. His involves 48 strung instruments playing every quarter-tone in two octaves, and the resulting sound is an extraordinary thing to experience. It's full of inconsistencies, little variations and flutters of tone that are the by-product of all these people performing collectively, and struggling to reproduce perfect, blank, white noise. It's a beautiful sound because of all these tiny flaws.

I hope this isn't reading like a reactionary rejection of electronics, like some pompous defence of the symphonic form. My life revolves around programming laptops, posting on Max/MSP forums, plugging things into amps. I love it all, and wouldn't give it up for anything. And musical epiphanies and obsessions have, of course, happened to me from recordings. And yet — I have a problem with microphones and speakers. My heart always sinks when I go to an orchestral concert and see speakers either side of the stage. It's such a compromise, a way of both simplifying and diluting the complexity of sounds. It's louder, but that's all.

Perhaps this is just a long way of saying that speakers

just aren't good enough yet. Certainly not good at putting across something as complicated as 48 individual sound sources. And not just in the concert hall: I love lots of classical recordings, but there's a belief that recordings are now somehow better than the 'real thing': there's no coughing, more volume, less mistakes. Look at my box sets, my hard drive with every recording of every symphony. I fell for this, too: I liked the idea that anyone can put an orchestra right in their front room (if you have spent enough on your hi-fi) and I was happy to accept this view of recording — until I saw this Penderecki concert.

Penderecki's music suffers more than most in the reduction from 48 instruments to two speakers — it really doesn't sound like that when you're in the room with it — but then, neither does a string quartet, or a solo voice. Listen to how they really sound, starting up from silence in a quiet room. It's been liberating for me to accept that you can't exactly reproduce an acoustic event with microphones and speakers: it makes the process of recording music a different endeavour, one that is focused on repeatability, and treats the studio like an enormous musical instrument instead of just a process of reproducing the sounds that are fed into it. You can't create an illusion of the real thing — so don't bother. It's liberating: an invitation to let any transformation take place.

By contrast, the live concert becomes this weird, collective effort to produce something that simply disappears into the air — and when there are no electronics involved, I find it an even stranger experience. But then, I'm greedy enough to want both: but think it more exciting to treat the two things — a concert and a recording — as utterly unrelated.

Jonny Greenwood is a UK composer and member of Radiohead

DAVID **GRUBBS** ON THE SEISMIC SHOCK OF SHORT PERFORMANCES

Short performances. Extremely brief ones.

I have been witness to a number of over-before-you-know-it performances that hit me with the force of an epiphany. Together they add up to a valuable lesson that I have yet to fully comprehend. Let me give a couple of examples.

It is the autumn of 1990, and I have just moved to Chicago. The place to play for indie post-punk groups is the Ukrainian Village's cosy Czar Bar. It seems a friendly enough scene, not especially venomous. A good many of the folks hanging out at the Czar Bar on a given Friday night grew up in straight edge hardcore groups. It's that kind of whole-someness. Into this milieu Drag City drops its third release, Royal Trux's hazy, confusing, monumentally feel-bad *Twin Infinitives*. In the weeks before Royal Trux are to play their first Chicago show, there's a lot of back and forth about *Twin Infinitives* being a major smokescreen, something of a farce. Regardless, everyone is talking about it, and on the evening of the show the Czar Bar is packed with people ready to call Royal Trux's bluff.

Neil and Jennifer from Royal Trux look like they're visiting from another planet. Planet Junk. They're tall ghosts, ill-to-the-gills hypothetical rock stars, and couldn't be more dissimilar in appearance and affect from the dressed down, commonsensical Midwestern folk. Royal Trux are malevolent spirits. They haunt the Czar Bar during the opening two acts. Then it's their turn, and of course they're nowhere to be found. 30 minutes pass, 40, perhaps more. Dead time that is to a gig what dead air is to radio. I remember being aware that live music had to stop at 1am. At probably 12:45, Neil and Jennifer roll back into the club to confront a hostile audience. Neil straps on a guitar and kickstarts a reel-to-reel deck that stutters forth an especially canned sounding recording of what I took to be cut-ups of The Master Musicians Of Joujouka. There's a little riffing, a little checking of the mic, the beginning of an attitudinal, non-sequiturish lyric. They slog through a couple of songs, but the monochromatic backing collage makes it all seem like one piece — and then the PA is shut off. It must be 1am, but the yanking of the plug feels unavoidably like a value judgment. Like being kicked off *The Gong Show*. Jennifer starts hollering 'LET US PLAY! LET! US! PLAY!' The show had come to an end. Elapsed time? I could be proven wrong, but I'm guessing that it lasted about ten minutes. I was thunderstruck. They had trashed the convention of the 40 minute set with narcotized aplomb and zero self-congratulation. None of the pro forma niceties of in theory giving people what they've paid for. In the decade after that night at the Czar Bar, I saw Royal Trux play numerous generally very good rock shows. But I never saw them — nor anyone else — pull off anything comparably disastrous and educational.

I've described that show to a number of people. At a party in Los Angeles someone responded with a similar tale of a Germs gig in which Darby Crash pulls over the lighting rig during the first song and then the show is over. That in turn disinterred my own memory of GG Allin's soundcheck prior to his opening for my group Squirrel Bait in the summer of 1986. Short version: GG's manager Bloody Mess plays a hissy cassette of backing tracks over the PA, GG climbs an unoccupied ladder, knocks it over, crashes to the ground, jumps up and tackles Brian McMahan, the club shuts off the PA and threatens to throw GG out. Elapsed time? About a minute.

When MTV began, I had a theory that its airtime would become so valuable that record companies would conspire to make commercial pop songs shorter and shorter. Top 40 hits would revert to girl group-era brevity before eventually winding up like the one minute jingles on The Residents' *Commercial Album*. Wishful thinking.

Here's another example of a brief, instructive performance. The Star Pine's Cafe, Tokyo, early 21st century. It's a Sunday afternoon show of solo, duo, and trio performances with improvising musicians Otomo Yoshihide, Sachiko M, Taku Sugimoto, Seiichi Yamamoto, Noël Akchoté, Quentin Rollet and myself. The first set is comprised of brief solos, all under ten minutes. Being constitutionally inclined towards music served in small, concentrated portions, this is a dream. (I also am drawn to savagely overlong performances, but that's another epiphany.) All of the solos were pleasurable affairs, but Taku Sugimoto's was The Lesson. This was at the front end of Taku's music being characterised by long stretches of inaction. The time that I had seen him prior to this he was playing in a lyrical, broken down, blues-like idiom. The Star Pine's performance starts with amp buzz. Preparations commence: three alligator clips are produced and carefully clamped onto the strings. A discarded string is slowly woven through the standard six. A percussion mallet is selected, considered, and rejected. A second mallet is brought out, and it appears to pass muster. I think about the fact that I've seen all kinds of performances of 'prepared' instruments but never a performance of the act of preparing. Unexpectedly, Taku strikes the body of his guitar in three different spots, and it's as if we've heard a comparison between three distinctly different bells. Having executed this sudden florescence, Taku slowly begins to disassemble his preparations. One senses that the performance has crested its midpoint, and that we're turning to head for the barn. Somewhat as expected, it takes the same length of time to remove the preparations. Slightly more sound is produced in the mirror action of disassemblage. The end is cued visually. Elapsed time? Eight minutes.

I know that perfection has no place in music, but this palindromic gesture was as perfect as they come, whatever that means.

David Grubbs is a US musician, label runner, academic and writer

In the faculty library where I studied for an undergraduate
degree in music, next to a bound collection of operatic arias
by the forgotten French Baroque composer André Campra, is
a not particularly well-worn copy of Cornelius Cardew's 193
page graphic score *Treatise*, first published in 1967. I found
and borrowed it in November 2007, following a summer spent
swatting up on semiotics and assorted theories of musical
meaning and communication. Having already spent some
time with 20th century experimental music, I did have some
idea of who Cardew was, and I had seen a page or two of the
score captured in a few textbooks and musical encyclopedias,
put there largely in their capacity as an entertaining visual
example of the extremes of notational creativity. A brief
mention in a lecture prompted me to actually look the
composition up — again, initially just for a bit of fun — and
when I did I was taken aback to find something so extensive
and diverse: so heavy.

The score is presented in a thin landscape format that
makes its contents appear as if viewed in widescreen, and yet
the size is slightly smaller than A4. Each page is filled with
meticulous and mystifying structures of thin black lines,
drawn using either a ruler, a compass, or occasionally a free
hand. Simultaneously scientific and playful, logical and
chaotic, these constructions are actually 'the music itself' (a
term us budding musicologists were warned against adopting
uncritically). This was despite — but yet somehow because
of — their unique and totally absorbing visual appeal. Indeed,
running constantly underneath these complex images are a
pair of conventionally notated staves that are left curiously
empty. Perhaps 'the music itself' wasn't really there at all.

You see, Cardew provides absolutely no instruction as
to how performers should translate *Treatise's* fascinating
pictograms into musical sound, and it's certainly far from
universally obvious exactly how the score's lines, curves and
dots could become specific sonic events. Strictly speaking,

there isn't even any suggestion in the volume that what you're holding is in fact a musical score rather than, say, a picture book of Constructivist sketches. The only clues are Cardew's wider career as a composer and, possibly, the music faculty's stamp on the inside cover. Yet as a starting point for musical activity, *Treatise* could conceivably result in an infinite number of different performances. As Cardew himself put it in the *Treatise Handbook*, which was next along on the bookshelf, '*Treatise* tells what it is like to manipulate sounds in composition.' It offers all of music and none of it, not seeming to actually be music at all.

It also intrigued me to find that the work was bound in exactly the same way as the hundreds of more traditional scores in the library, including the Campra collection — as a fabric-covered hardback (in this case navy blue) with gold embossed capital letters along the spine, announcing merely, 'CARDEW — TREATISE'. Presented in this way, it was as if the library and the centuries-long, canonical tradition represented therein had accepted it as a legitimate work, no more or less deserving of study and performance than a Mozart concerto or a Beethoven symphony. As such, it modestly seemed to offer just another example of musical possibility.

Cardew's *Treatise* is more than just another score, however. It warmed me to see it bound and on the library's shelves because it does push musical possibility to such an extreme extent. Specifically, *Treatise* is a treatise on notation's outermost limits as well as a comprehensive account of visual forms that we infer will give rise to musical forms. By remaining in the visual domain, it freezes 193 utterly bizarre sonic structures, leaving them to kindle the imagination even as they lie forever just out of our reach, as idealist essences. And in fact, we come to realise, all scores are like this. *Treatise* shows that notation contains no greater musical truth, no more privileged access to 'the music itself', than do the vagaries of performance.

For me, *Treatise*'s power lies in its dual role as a philosophical lesson on communication and interpretation, and an idealist promise of strange musical performances in the unknown future. I've never had any interest in hearing *Treatise* interpreted on CD, unless I were sure of perceiving the performers' process on the same level of detail I enjoy in the score. But even then, why take the trouble when 'the music itself' would seem to be right there on the page? The closely mingling orbs on page three, seeming like satellite photographs of extraterrestrial industry, have a peaceful and warming tone. Pages 24 and 25 hint at utopian living with their perfect blend of perpendicular straight lines and undulating, rounded surfaces. The noisy 'black pages' culminate in the deafening, gong-like giant note-head on page 133. An explosion on page 155 sends shards of minim flying in all directions, and on page 190 (my favourite), thick, freely drawn expressionist lines burst out of the staves and pile together like a fiery sunrise, while two crows circle overhead. Perhaps you would deny that any of this is really a 'musical' experience, and I would ask you, why?

Returning to *Treatise* four years later, having cited it as an example of an 'alien genre' (defined as 'an entirely new way of practising music') in my book *Infinite Music*, I can see that the work and its handbook had influenced me more than I could actually recall. In his handbook notes, Cardew suggests that a musician 'might use *Treatise* as a path to the ocean of spontaneity'. This is exactly the metaphor I unknowingly chose at the climax of *Infinite Music's* first part, where I imagine the melting down of music's formal strictures as leaving a vast 'sea of variability', and each individual musical variable as a path trodden by the imaginations of composers towards this state. Cardew's demoralised observation that 'just as you find your sounds are too alien, intended 'for a different culture', you make the same discovery about your beautiful notation: no one is willing to understand it' must have been a precursor to my own more cautiously optimistic thoughts on what I called 'alien styles', with their xenophile languages and the challenges they pose to listeners.

Treatise could be viewed as an entire musical tradition in itself, and it's a shame that few other composers engaged with its mysterious visual music making methods. Unlike

Campra's operatic arias and the hundreds of such volumes in the library, we can't situate its stylistic quirks in relation to a community of similar voices. Cardew was one of a few lone astronauts in musical space, but I believe his work will have encircled centuries of future musical creativity.

Adam Harper is a UK musicologist and critic

A saving grace of my last year in a Canadian university town
was the dialogue which I enjoyed with my film professor. He
was not only an English hippy intellectual, whose stridently
leftist bent was signalled by the red ceramic stars adorning
each ear, he was also a hedonist. The best looking women in
the lecture hall gravitated to his leonine form and, so far as I
could tell, he accommodated them all. I lusted after his job.

With my professor's dubious example, I had already
picked Kenneth Anger, the notorious American avant garde
film maker and author, as the subject of my thesis. I collected
materials relating to the allegedly Satanic artist, including a
set of programme notes for his *Magick Lantern Cycle* — being
all of Anger's films screened end to end — which alluded to
a hidden subtext visible to those audience members who had
taken LSD. I shouldn't have been surprised at my mentor's
response. 'If you're really serious about this thesis, you'd
better do it. Anger clearly intended them to be seen that way.'
Seeing how he offered to pick up the tab for both the acid and
the Anger films, this trip was going to be difficult to refuse.

Up to then, my familiarity with drugs extended to
aspirin and antihistamine. Taking on what the late Derek
Taylor referred to as 'the old heaven and hell drug' required
a considerable leap of faith. My formative concert-going
experiences had taken place ten years before, in the hippy
venues of Detroit. LSD didn't seem to do anyone much good.
The audiences' animal-pack behaviour, the interminable
guitar and drum solos, and the clothing comprised a checklist
of contra-indications.

Still, I was forced to concede the point. Anger's own
programme notes spelled it out on burnt orange paper.
'Psychedelic researchers desirous to Turn On for *Pleasure
Dome* should absorb their sugar cubes at this point.' Who was
I to get cold feet, and disappoint my academic mentor over an
issue as trifling as my mental health?

Come the appointed day, I turned up at the Aladdin's

cave my professor called home. For someone so vocally Marxist, he certainly loved things. More a Victorian museum, the house was crammed floor to ceiling with vintage magic posters, souvenirs from African expeditions, Ian Hamilton Finlay sculptures and, best of all, shelves full of vinyl esoterica.

It was at the house that I'd met Kenneth Anger some months before, at a post-screening party held in his honour. He was charming and bitchy by turns, as one might expect of the author of *Hollywood Babylon*, dispensing film history arcana and dirt on The Rolling Stones in equal measure. He was quick to remind anyone within earshot that Charles Manson was responsible for the disappearance of Anger's magnum opus, *Lucifer Rising*. I thought about that as I ate the two squares of acid-impregnated blotter paper handed me by my professor. Before downing some of the blotter himself, he set the *Magick Lantern Cycle* running through a 16 mm projector.

To be honest, we didn't get that far with it. Waiting for our perceptions to be cleaned (I had read Huxley, if only not to feel like a complete greenhorn), the stereo beckoned. Several new releases were auditioned. Records which were reputedly made 'under the influence' seemed over busy and cynical. Brian Jones's *Pipes Of Pan At Joujouka* simply scared the crap out of me; but then, it had done the same five years earlier when I first brought it home and listened to it sober.

David Bowie's *Low* had come out that day. I'd been looking forward to hearing the results of Bowie's first collaboration with Brian Eno. *Another Green World, Discreet Music* and sundry Cluster albums had been in heavy rotation on the professorial stereo in months past. As the eves of the house grew deeper, and the walls darker, *Low* was revealed in all its icy glory. We both immediately lost interest in the *Magick Lantern Cycle*, with its overcooked Cocteau references. Why couldn't we just watch Fritz Lang's *Spione*, all clean lines and minimal frame compositions, with *Low* as its high-tension soundtrack?

Replaying the instrumentals 'A New Career In A New Town' and 'Art Decade', we obsessed on the gated drum sounds, never suspecting they were a foretaste of an approaching syndrum plague. Eno's abrasive 'splinter Mini-Moog', the paint-by-numbers quality of the 'tape' cellos and horns, and the rhythm section's mechanistic funk added up to something like Pop Art. We agreed that 'Always Crashing In The Same Car', with its shimmering guitars wafting upwards like the heat from a highway's blacktop, felt like a Richard Hamilton canvas. At this point, the living room curtains achieved a life of their own.

And so it went through the night. My professor wondered why anyone would bother with the lyrics, when these marvellous textures lay just beneath the surface. He snapped a Polaroid of the speaker's grille cloth, to emphasise the point. So began the 'texture-supplants-melody' thread in our discussions. That, and much ongoing humour which only made sense to the two of us. There was added lustre and depth to our friendship through the next few months, until the English hippy who counted Foucault and U-Roy as equal role models was knocked off his bicycle and killed the following summer.

Mine would not be the definitive study of Anger and his films. I'd had the stuffing knocked out of my enthusiasm for the temperamental creator and his 'magick' cycle during that vibrant evening in 1977. The following year, I gave a lecture at a Buffalo art gallery in upstate New York, communicating my own excitement about the texture-in-pop issue. The gallery had a great sound system, too: the neighbours called the police.

'That world! These days it's all been erased and they've rolled it up like a scroll and put it away somewhere. Yes I can touch it with my fingers. But where is it?' In the epilogue to his chimerical short story 'Emergency', Denis Johnson sums up the complexity of my memories of that time, an amalgam of nostalgia and amazement and a newfound joy in the fabric of sounds. I was not destined to be a film professor. As it turned out, I'd found a new career in a new town.

Richard Henderson is a US film music editor and supervisor

Epiphanies ruin everything, all the while leaving everything
intact. The world you once knew has now gone for good, yet
still it refuses to lie in ruins before you. It is consequently in
the nature of an epiphany to illuminate its subject rather than
the other way round. Its significance remains reflected at
best. I can't imagine anyone wanting to stand for too long in
so treacherous a light, but that's probably just me.

I first heard Martin Denny's 'Quiet Village' on 29
November 1981 in the front room of the Manchester
apartment of the music critic Jon Savage. It was a Sunday
afternoon. Biting Tongues — the group I was in — had
performed live at Rafters the night before and Savage
had been in the audience, along with some members of A
Certain Ratio. Jon had been impressed enough by the show
to invite us over the following day for lunch. That's how
my bandmates Graham Massey, Howard Walmsley and
I found ourselves perched on various pieces of furniture
around the room watching Savage jump from one stack of
vinyl to another, pulling out various recordings he wanted
us to hear. It was all vintage stuff, mostly original pressings,
but presented with the manic hyper-kinetic intensity of an
arcade coin-op reaching its final level. Jon doesn't play you
just one track at time: you get three or four at once. A 45 rpm
pressing of Sandy Nelson's 'Let There Be Drums' gets yanked
off the turntable to make room for 'Boss Hoss' by The Sonics,
while a muted cassette recording of an early La Monte Young
performance continues to unwind itself unsteadily in the
background.

Then Savage picks up an LP in a damaged cardboard
sleeve, held together by a badly scuffed polythene jacket.
'Do any of you know this?' he asks. On the front cover a girl
stares with eerie, enigmatic poise through the opening in a
bead curtain. The teardrop-shaped pendant decorating her
brow speaks of strange ports of call, while her red lipstick is
pure Fifth Avenue. The word *Exotica* floats calmly above her

in thin white capitals. I'm hooked already and I haven't even heard a note yet.

Such casually studied tat was of supreme importance back then. We spent a lot of time and energy seeking out things that no longer seemed to fit, that were untouched by familiarity and that had somehow allowed themselves to become displaced from the surroundings in which they found themselves: *Man From UNCLE* paperbacks, *Jackie* annuals, unauthorised Elvis biographies, 1950s pornographic novels, *Mars Attacks!* trading cards... And yet none of these had prepared me for what I am about to encounter.

First the sound of frogs croaking, then the trilling of some tropical bird: both of them flagrantly artificial, obviously mocked up in the studio. Accompanied by prominent Latin percussion, a piano trickles and tinkles its way sedately through a melody that will soon become indelibly etched into my memory. And why? Because the tropical bird in the background won't shut up. In fact, it seems to have awakened half the jungle by now and the man responsible for all the wildlife impersonations is busily throwing himself into convulsions. It's not until approximately one minute and 47 seconds into the song that the epiphany takes place. As if to mark some gentle climax in the tune, a vibraphone chimes in unexpectedly, catching me completely off guard. I start laughing hysterically. It is the greatest thing I have ever heard in my life. Across the room Graham's eyes are shining.

'Jon, what *is* this?'

'Martin Denny. Gen [ie Genesis P-Orridge] passed it on to me. Boyd Rice [aka NON] gave it to him when Throbbing Gristle were in San Francisco. Then he found a copy with a better sleeve, so he gave this one to me.'

It is traditional, of course, to laugh only when history repeats itself for a second time. When it comes to exotic easy listening, as with any modern phenomenon firmly grounded in the false and the artificial, the reverse is nearly always true. The first response is hilarity and only then does the true gravity of the experience manifest itself.

Compared with Les Baxter's original version of 'Quiet Village' on his 1951 *Ritual Of The Savage* album, Denny's arrangement is a slow paced, sultry affair. Subsequent renditions recorded over the years, including that on his 1969 *Exotic Moog* album, are slower and sultrier still. It's the first, however, laid down in mono at Webley Edwards's Honolulu studio at the end of Denny's residency at the Shell Bar in Henry J Kaiser's Hawaiian Village hotel complex in 1956, which remains the cultural lodestone. A work of tranquil alien beauty, all of pop's stale orthodoxies stand exposed in its presence. Luxurious, irrational and counterfeit, it challenges you to hear things in quite the same way ever again.

Once your perceptions shift, however, they cannot go back to the way they once were. That's also in the nature of an epiphany. From that moment on, Graham Massey and I started collecting Martin Denny recordings with a fanaticism that scares me to this day. We dug through sale racks and secondhand bins, swapped tapes of rarities, sat up late into the night studying sleevenotes and comparing recording details. August Colón, the majestically named South American percussionist responsible for the exotic birdcalls and related sound effects, became a hero of mythological dimensions to us. Pretty soon we were also buying anything we could find by Les Baxter and former Denny sideman Arthur Lyman, who had played the vibes on the earliest versions of 'Quiet Village'. Then came Milt Raskin, Tak Shindo, Felix Slatkin, Nelson Riddle, Esquivel, Yma Sumac, Cong Ling, The Randy Van Horn Singers...

Except such listening pleasures no longer seem as removed from their surroundings as they did back in the early 1980s. A large part of techno is, after all, the continuation of exotica in another form. Graham made that connection quite plain by the decade's end in his work with 808 State. Listen again to 'Pacific State' or just about any other track on *Ninety*, and you'll see what I mean.

Shortly after my first exposure to 'Quiet Village', Savage and I meet by chance on a crowded London street. Christmas is only a few days away. 'I'm glad we ran into each other,' he says. 'It'll save me the bother of mailing this to you.' Then he hands me the copy of *Exotica* in the damaged sleeve, still in its protective polythene jacket. 'I found one in better condition a few days ago,' he says. 'And you seemed to enjoy it so much, I thought you might like to have it. Merry Christmas.'

Ken Hollings is a UK writer and broadcaster

Teenage romantics, obsessive fans of the elusive form of
music by necessity, walk right into the myths of the preceding
generation — myths that lie like a fog. On anyone's terms, the
rock mythology of the 1970s — the collusion of benumbed
journalists and the walking dead glitterati — was a veritable
pea-souper. Actual members of that generation probably
fared better at wafting aside the hype, coming to more
reasonable conclusions. Those of us growing up in the 1980s,
unlucky enough to have missed the actual incarnation of
these gods in their heyday, didn't stand a chance.

Aged 19 in 1990, I had already been fixated on the
legendary rock music of the 70s for half a decade or more. The
Lester Bangs compendium *Psychotic Reactions And Carburetor
Dung* (1988) was a talisman, and I had followed its trail to
Greil Marcus's *Mystery Train* (first published in 1977). Now a
student at London's Camberwell Art School, I was unleashed
in the capital with the opportunity to attend concerts.

None of us were really rockers or ravers at this point
in time, although you couldn't tell this by looking at the
iconography of the era. Purist distinctions came much later.
This confusion in the audience was what baggy was about.
What united everyone was drugs, usually taken before
breakfast until you collapsed at the other end of the day. Not
today's obligatory cocaine and hydroponic weed, mind, but
a filthy cocktail of the altogether messier hash, mushrooms,
acid and ecstasy. These 'foolish' drugs certainly made a mess
of me. One thing led to another and I ended up on crutches.

Undeterred by this disability, I continued to go to gigs.
Waif-thin, usually coughing up prodigious amounts of mucus,
with a half-deranged glint in my eye, I would limp to shows
on sticks. I was often alone, as friends couldn't be bothered
to tear themselves from the bong and gas-fire. Long a veteran
of blagging my way backstage, now a practising art student,
I had stuff to give away once there. Nursing a romantic
disaster, I had holed up at the Brixton house of one of the

original supermodels, a famous beauty who had taken pity on me, and while living there worked up a book of illustrations to TS Eliot's *The Love Song Of J Alfred Prufrock*. I was pleased with the work and wanted my heroes to see it.

My first quarry was Wire, or Wir, as they had temporarily become, then touring one of their weaker LPs, *Manscape* (1990). Backstage at some dive at the foot of the North End Road, I remember Graham Lewis looking impossibly dapper and Colin Newman examining me wryly as I hobbled into their dressing room — the wrong kind of groupie. These guys were as mysterious as it got. I was not disappointed. I still wonder, if it made its way out of the dressing room, what they thought of my Eliot book?

Alex Chilton came next, at the University of London Union. Another 70s legend, at that point in time his reputation was riding impossibly high. How I, a gammy cretin, worked my way backstage I will never know. Chilton had something of an entourage and, after accepting the book of illustrations in a flippant but basically appreciative way, asked me to join them. I remember a very pretty girl, probably the same age as me. Chilton rolled a joint and offered me a puff and I'll always regret turning him down (what was I thinking?). Alex was the very picture of the cool, wild rock star. May he rest in peace.

My ebook, *100 Lost Rock Albums From The 1970s*, is a self-styled 'final word'. It's my attempt to sink nails into my obsession with the 70s. In the same way that hauntology should have outgrown this era, so I reckon the writing has long been on the wall for the culture-wide fixation on 70s rock. Simon Reynolds's *Retromania*, with its gently persuasive critique, has rightfully called time on all manner of retro-fixations. Tom Verlaine features at the tail end of my ebook. I pick up his 1979 debut for reconsideration, and it was Verlaine who was the last recipient of my *Prufrock* illustrations.

A Jon Wilde interview in *Melody Maker* from May 1990, archived online, reveals that Tom Verlaine played 'a couple of solo acoustic gigs at London's Bloomsbury Theatre'. I only remember descending a great many stairs on crutches; holding onto the handrail, pausing, then descending further and further for what seemed like forever. Pushing open a door, I entered a very quiet, evenly lit, mirrored dressing room. Verlaine, tall and thin, was leaning against a chair with his arms folded, talking quietly to a woman. No attitudes, no outfits, no drugs, no entourage, no hubbub. He greeted me smiling and in an easy, relaxed manner, was delighted with my rough-hewn gift and asked lots of questions about the pictures. I remember being completely thrown off guard by his gentility and openness. This wasn't some remote deity; a genius, perhaps, but just another human being, just another artist.

Matthew Ingram is a UK music critic, graphic designer and animator

VIJAY IYER ON A SINGLE MYSTICAL CHORD PLAYED BY THE PIANIST CECIL TAYLOR

There was a period in the early-mid-1990s when I listened non-stop to Cecil Taylor — seeing him live often, and dosing myself with his recordings every morning over breakfast. On the live solo double album *Garden* (1982), 'Pemmican', one of Taylor's many great, inimitable solo ballads, particularly grabbed me. It's such a beautiful song. Plus, it had one of the most transparent and economical forms I'd ever heard from Taylor. In an apparent nod to standard jazz practice, he plays the head twice, seemingly improvises over the song's progression, and plays the head out again.

One chord he plays changed my life. It's in the middle of the head, one minute in (and recurs on the repeats); a mysterious and spectral sound, stable, pure, yet somehow void. I set to work at the piano, trying to discern its contents: OK, we've got an A octave in the bass, and an octave B in the right hand, a G in the middle there... That's it? In three notes I was suddenly peering into the abyss.

Sure, the same chord may occur elsewhere, for example in the midst of a typical montuno pattern, but here it was frozen in mid-flight and seen perspicuously from all angles, like an airborne character in *The Matrix*. This cluster wasn't mere harmony; it was physics, philosophy, poetics, architecture. The chord had mathematical symmetry (surrounding the root by whole steps on either side); it had physical grounding (the first, seventh and ninth partials of the harmonic series); it displayed no clear tonal function (having no third or fifth); and as a sound it lacked nothing, wanted and needed nothing. To my 23 year old ears, this was an anti-chord. I could listen to this sound all day; I wanted to live inside it, learn from it; it had something I didn't have.

I suddenly started noticing the sonority everywhere. Andrew Hill deployed it in his trio tune 'Subterfuge' on the classic *Black Fire*. Ellington, Monk and Randy Weston hinted at it, and maybe James Brown and Bernie Worrell knew, too. I started experimenting with that chord in my own playing, but it always sounded wrong. Like a child with a new word, I wielded it inappropriately, trying it out on standards, in rock and hiphop groups, at weddings and funerals.

Soon afterward I found myself participating in Taylor's creative orchestra music. I was living in Oakland, California, and was still playing occasional gigs on violin, which had been my first instrument, though I kept saying I had quit. But I had to say yes to this occasion, in which 40 West Coast musicians studied and interpreted Taylor's work under his guidance. In rehearsals, Taylor initially seemed a stickler for detail. We spent the first three hour rehearsal on one postage stamp-sized corner of one of his handwritten scores; he would rework the material bit by bit, singing or conducting a phrase for us, or asking us to permute the written pitches in a certain way. Early on, when asked about the role of the written material, he said: this is the formal content of the piece; what I want is for all the players to bring their individual languages to its interpretation and execution.

As the week progressed, his guidance grew less direct; eventually he would just set us in motion and leave the room. I realised that somehow he had taught us aspects of his language — his sense of phrasing and repetition, the way he rigorously explodes a line. Now we were to bring our own ideas and actions to this context. When he returned to the rehearsal room, he would find that we had made something out of his scores. A real collective bond formed; we were not just an orchestra, but a small civilization.

Unsurprisingly, in performance we experienced a civilization's worth of strife and tension. It all came to pass on 26 October 1995, my 24th birthday, the date of a now legendary concert by this shortlived ensemble-cum-cult at the San Francisco Jazz Festival. Once we'd settled onstage after a semi-choreographed opening ritual, we found ourselves in baffled disagreement as to what was supposed to be happening or what to do next.

Confronted by the absence of a more linear score to which to adhere or any direct commands from the leader (Taylor functioning more as a trickster in the ensemble), many musicians immediately abandoned their allegiance to the brittle orchestral aesthetic we had developed in rehearsals, opting instead for the more predictable ecstatic wailing. It became an issue of physical power, the softer instruments subjected to the louder players' whims. In response, small, localised factions formed to conduct their own unified activities, creating pockets of apparent order in the mêlée. The performance included many such flashes of beauty, fortuitous moments of focus interspersed amid at times inscrutable orchestral noise.

After what felt like an age of war, the ensemble's energy was expended, and the evening ended with a consummate, almost prayerful unaccompanied statement from Taylor, coming to rest on, yes, that chord again — quieting our quickened hearts, healing our battle wounds, absolving our sins.

I came to understand that the message of this chord is one of peace. It doesn't even ask to be heard; it has an uncommon stillness, as though it had coexisted with humanity for millennia, as if it predates us and will outlast us. If such stillness could exist at the heart of a music as turbulent as Cecil Taylor's, that could only mean that I had previously misread his music. For all its animated surface qualities and its notorious tumult, Taylor's music somehow possesses a motionless, timeless interior; this chord was proof. I couldn't even conceive of his music as transgressive anymore; at moments like these, it seemed to exist as incontrovertible fact.

Vijay Iyer is a US pianist and composer

In 1987 I was 17 and a slicked back, tucked in, all present
and correct Scottish geek boy of the highest order. The high
point of my week would be hanging out at the Airdrie Library
astonomy club debating the end sequence of *2001: A Space
Odyssey*, repeat-spinning *Number Of The Beast*, and arguing
viciously over *Dr Who* minutiae. So how the hell I ever got to
hear about The Pastels I'll never know. I was hanging around
comic shops a lot and, at a guess, I'd say that I started picking
up Glasgow fanzines such as *Coca Cola Cowboy* and *Simply
Thrilled, Honey* after spotting them lurking on the shelves
of Virgin next to back issues of *Warrior* or something, back
in the days when the chainstore suckers still risked stocking
such non-corporate product.

Or maybe it was *Rock On Scotland* (since somewhat
disappointingly rechristened *Beat Patrol*), Radio Scotland's
weekly 120 minute delve into the Scottish underground,
which first hipped me to them. Whatever, I'd picked up
the 'Truck Train Tractor' single, my first ever non-metal
purchase, and I was hooked. They were playing a week on
Thursday at Fury Murrays on Maxwell Street, right by the
River Clyde. Now I had never been to a gig in my life. To me
this whole social scene was a frightening and mysterious
world populated by hipsters and women — the only time I
had previously expressed an interest in going to a gig, namely
AC/DC at The Apollo, my older metal mates had warned me
that it would be 'too rough'.

I asked my dad's advice. That's right, my dad, whose
last gig was Perry Como at a dancehall in Belfast sometime in
the 1950s. 'I'm thinking of going to a concert, dad, what are
they like, what should you, uh, wear?' Truly, I was clueless.
He soon straightened me out. At concerts, he said, it was
mostly couples, you wore a suit and tie, ordered some food
and watched the show from your table. OK, that sounded
about right to my sci-fi addled self, and I was soon kitted
out in one of my dad's favourite suits: green checks, yellow

hankie and tie set, pair of polished slip-ons, white socks. The business.

So my dad drives me in, parks outside the club and goes over to the door to make sure I get in all right, me with my pubic moustache and hanky trying to pass as over 18. No problem, we're through. The people start coming through the door and handing their tickets to my dad, thinking he's a bouncer. He's standing there straightfaced, taking people's tickets, when Peter Easton and Stuart Cruickshank from *Rock On Scotland* pile through. By this time, well into his new role, my dad takes their guest passes, shouting at some cloakroom girl to 'take these gentlemen's coats for them'. I swiftly pocketed the passes, which I'm sure got me in to see some tripe like The Weather Prophets the following week.

My dad finally stops taking tickets and running the cloakroom, and I say my goodbyes and descend into the venue. It's dark as hell but I'm starting to get the impression that my dad's idea of gig etiquette was, uh, a little wide of the mark. By about a mile. Everyone around me has Byrds bowlcuts and leathers, jeans and baseball boots, torn-up Ramones T-shirts and checked shirts. And they're all looking at me like I'd even fail an audition for bass player in The Lighthouse Family. Then I feel a hand on my shoulder. My dad's loose in the venue, standing next to me, offering me a Coke. My humiliation complete, I resign myself to the approaching nightmare. Just then he recognises Stephen Pastel in the crowd, no doubt from a picture I'd shown him, and slaps him on the back, shouting, 'Hi there, Stephen!' Stephen looks up at my dad like he'd just been flashed by a maniac.

The Vaselines were on stage first. They got there just before my dad, who'd climbed onto the side of the stage to carry on a conversation with a bouncer he had befriended, leaving me in relative peace to watch the show, with only the occasional 'Are you all right, son?' echoing round the room to contend with. The Vaselines were incredible — Frances was beautiful and Eugene was cool, like John Cale in motorpsycho boots. It was one of their first gigs, when they were still just dual voice and guitars, plus backing tapes, which Stephen Pastel recently described to me as sounding like 'The Shaggs trying to tone their exuberance down for a wedding'. Frances had trouble playing a D chord and Eugene was barking out titles like 'Up Your Arse' (a sadly unrecorded gem) and 'Son Of A Gun' to a sea of some of the best quality heckling I've had the privilege to experience.

The Pastels were something else altogether. Their effect on me was immediate and utterly overwhelming — a heroic dose of non-musicianly invention, inspirational rhetoric and staggered walls of blast furnace feedback. I'd never experienced volume like it. In fact, I had no idea that live groups played so loud, so when they all laid into the Velvets psych-mantra of 'Baby Honey', I felt my scalp peel back. The whole gig was a beautiful shambles with then guitarist Brian Superstar's amp packing in for a couple of songs, Stephen bursting strings, kids spilling onto the stage at Aggi's feet. Eugene of The Vaselines staggered on and added some screeching violin. For the first time I realised that here was something I could really be part of. The music spoke directly to my heart and moved me like no art or music had ever done before. And it was played by kids, kids who clearly had no musical training, who stood in the crowd and drank a beer before they went on, who walked down Byres Road on a Saturday, took a coffee in the Grosvenor, took art seriously enough to take it into their own hands to make a stand for idiosyncratic expression. There was a feeling of revolution in the air — the venue was sold out, with kids hanging from the walls and standing on tables. Glasgow was never the same for me after that; it became a mythical city of sun-stroked tenements and bohemian punk artists, of secret cafes and basement scams. They lit up the Glasgow night.

In fact, nothing was the same after that. My dad drove me home, unaware of the effect the night had had on me. As I dressed for bed I looked in the mirror and messed my hair up — I knew I'd never comb it again.

David Keenan is a Scottish music critic and author

STEWART LEE ON THE COMMON ABILITY OF GREAT
HUMOUR AND GREAT MUSIC TO SURPRISE

In March 1997, in the Purcell Room at London's South Bank
Centre, the UK guitarist Derek Bailey played alongside
the Japanese duo Ruins. I seem to recall a moment
where the septuagenarian genius, lost in concentration,
actually bumped into the back wall of the stage, his guitar
making a resonating clang. Looking down, he appeared to
consider what had happened, and then playfully bashed
the instrument into the wall a second time. I laughed, and
despite the wealth of different responses Bailey's music had
already offered me, I never thought it would provoke laughter.
But something great music shares with great comedy is the
capacity to surprise, to take us out of ourselves and engender
a joyous — and not necessarily mean spirited or cynical —
laughter. I've subsequently learned that Bailey once played
in the pit orchestra for British comedy duo Morecambe &
Wise when they toured theatres before their TV success in the
1960s and 70s. Banging your guitar into a wall by accident,
and then doing it again on purpose in a spirit of clownish
curiosity, seems to me like a classic Eric Morecambe move.

There's a great documentary about stand-up comedy
called *The Aristocrats*. Directed by Paul Provenza and Penn
Jillette, the film shows 60 or so stand-ups telling a shaggy
dog story enjoyed privately by American comics, but never
inflicted on the public. In essence, 'The Aristocrats', as
the gag is known, includes a central section which can
be infinitely expanded and altered, and goes like this. A
talent scout visits a Broadway booker to sell him a new
vaudeville act he has seen. It involves a husband and wife,
usually depicted dressed in formal finery, performing acts
of escalating obscene sexual violence on each other, then on
their children, and perhaps on any animals or birds in the
vicinity, to the accompaniment of sophisticated classical
music, or cabaret show tunes, or light opera, or whatever.
At the end of this description, which Gilbert Gottfried is
seen spinning out for over an hour, the baffled and sickened

booker says, 'That sounds appalling. I can't imagine why anyone would want to see that. What is this act called?', to which the talent scout replies, with a smile, or a wink, or an attitude of profound regret, or a showbiz snap of the fingers and thumbs: 'The Aristocrats.' It's hilarious. But perhaps you have to be there.

I've never subscribed to the idea that stand-up is, along with jazz and comic books, one of America's great 20th century artforms. This seems a blinkered and isolationist observation. But *The Aristocrats* started to swing me. Halfway through, soon after one of the comics has gone off on a tangent involving the father repeatedly slamming his penis in a drawer for the audience's edification, somebody makes a case for stand-up's relationship with jazz. The distinct variations different performers can extrapolate from 'The Aristocrats' tells us that stand-up is about 'the singer, not the song'. Just as John Coltrane's 'My Favorite Things' is different from the Julie Andrews version, so George Carlin's 'Aristocrats', told with a world-weariness that suggests he has been compelled against his will to relate this horrible event, differs vastly from Billy Connolly's, which is delivered with typically infectious relish.

Carlin, a 50s Catskills hack turned 60s radical turned elder statesman of American stand-up, wisely draws the distinction between 'shock', a term that comes with pejorative overtones, and 'surprise', which has no obvious moral dimension. Though the endless variations in different versions of 'The Aristocrats' mainly involve stacking up increasing levels of scatological or sexual symbols, what's really making us laugh is the pleasure of surprise, of things being simply unexpected and wrong, of reversing the usual order of things. Surprise is the reason a one year old child laughs if you put a shoe on your head. Shoes are for feet, not heads. Even a baby has a sense of inappropriate behaviour. Respectable looking families shouldn't smash their genitals into drawers on stage in the name of entertainment. And guitars shouldn't be banged repeatedly into walls by elderly musicians. But how exciting it is to not know what's going to happen next. Sometimes Derek Bailey's music makes me feel like a kid on a rollercoaster. And Carlin, like some Native American shaman-clown, makes the need to subvert expectation, to continually surprise, sound like an artist's holy obligation.

It seems to me there are two broadly different approaches to stand-up, and by association to all art, each with their own strengths. At commercial British comedy chains like Jongleurs or the Comedy Store, performers tell you about your life, and things that always happen to you, and you may feel comforted by this. Go beyond the usual venues and you may see acts advance ideas that would not normally have occurred to you. In his book *Improvisation*, Derek Bailey assumes a position in opposition to the very act of musical composition itself. But there's a kind of social need both for songs we can all sing, and for jokes about buses always being late, and men being different from women. Only the most extreme avant gardist would deny the value of all-embracing, utilitarian art. It's just that all-embracing, utilitarian art tends to be a bit shit. When millions wept for their own mortality after the death of Princess Diana, all they were offered was an Elton John song with the words changed a bit.

Great art, whether it's laboriously crafted or spontaneously generated, tends towards the surprise factor that Carlin describes, and Bailey embodies. Derek Bailey is bold enough to refuse to gloss his work with emotional signifiers, just as George Carlin doesn't tell jokes as if they're supposed to be funny. Both make us do the work, and we get the reward of appearing to surprise ourselves. But the breakthrough moment, for me, of seeing Bailey bash his guitar into the back wall of the Purcell Room, was realising that I could be made to laugh, against my will, in an atmosphere of high seriousness, in the temple of culture, by the simple childlike joy of surprise. Derek Bailey, it seemed, was giving me permission to laugh.

Stewart Lee is a UK stand-up comedian

ALAN LICHT ON EDDIE VAN HALEN'S GUITAR PYROTECHNICS

Being a DJ is probably a good way to get through adolescence. Being a guitar hero is too, believe me. But either way the competition is stiff. In America the high school rock scene can be a lot like sports or gunslinging: there's always someone who's 'the best' and someone trying to become 'the best'.

In 1981, at the age of 13, I was playing guitar in a group called The Fuddruckers. One day the other guitarist in the group played me a tape of Eddie Van Halen's 90 second solo guitar extravaganza 'Eruption', recorded in 1978. Generally I was able to duplicate solos by ear, no matter how fast — Clapton, Page, Hendrix, whoever — but the final section of 'Eruption' was another matter. What the hell was he doing? A blinding, Paganini-damaged cadenza/blitzkrieg, Van Halen's playing instantly exploded the guitar's limits; old standards of 'speed' were out the window.

The gauntlet had been thrown down; this was state of the art shit. I had the same reaction ten years later when I heard Keiji Haino for the first time (too bad Haino's never hooked up with David Lee Roth, although it's never too late). Later an older teenage friend showed me and my fellow guitarist how it was done: two handed tapping on the fretboard. We both learned how to play 'Eruption' note for note. From then on tapping became de rigueur for keeping up with the Joneses as a teenage guitar whiz. My counterpart in The Fuddruckers became obsessed with it, and a rivalry ensued. Unlike him I thought there was more to music than metal guitar, but he was unconvinced — he threw my copy of the first Clash album at the wall at one point. So we sacked him.

A new group, Shattered Glass, rose from the ashes of The Fuddruckers, and we did a lot of Van Halen covers. I was able to pick out most of Eddie's solos by ear, which earned me high regard at the time. It was determined that the introduction to 'Little Guitars' was impossible to play, but I figured it out; same for 'Spanish Fly' (the acoustic

'Eruption' on *Van Halen II*). Perhaps most memorable was my replication of Eddie's solo on Michael Jackson's 'Beat It', executed flawlessly until the final note which was a half step sharp (documented on a rehearsal tape from the time).

Of course later I learned about Hans Reichel and Fred Frith, who were doing much more sophisticated investigations of two-hand tapping in the early 1970s in the name of 'extended technique'. Then Stanley Jordan and Michael Hedges came out with complex chordal approaches to the method, but none of these was as exciting, as significant, as Eddie. He took it to the kids, he did it in the name of speed and flash. 'Eruption' had the effect of a souped up racing car. He stole the crown from the 60s guitar gods, made them — for a time — look out of date. In that sense 'Eruption' was punk rock (which he hated). Before Eddie, just running up and down blues scales was enough to make you 'good'. After 'Eruption' it was a whole new ball game, harmonically. It made the solos in 'Freebird' sound just as ridiculous as The Germs or The Adverts did. Suddenly you had kids using all the modes in solos; eventually you had groups like Slayer taking totally atonal solos at lightning speed. As a 90 second tantrum, 'Eruption' also parallels the punk and no wave singles of the era. In an interview Eddie said he never structured his solos, they came right off the top of his head. A free improvisor and a punk!

Flash and technique have always been disparaged by post-punk sensibilities, yet growing up, unlike Joe Strummer or Kevin Shields or whoever, I never listened to these guys and thought: I could never do that. I always thought I could, and I did. I worshipped guitarists but in a way I never put them on a pedestal. After all they had the same six strings and 24 frets that I had, if they could do it, why not me? I never felt limited by anything. Whatever 'outside' playing techniques I've cultivated over the years has been despite my ability to play conventionally, not because of an inability to play that way. I listened to 'I Heard Her Call My Name' back then as much as I listened to 'Eruption' and I still can't play that solo note for note: I appreciated that in my teens too. And then there's Jeff Beck, who can be noisy, tasteful, melodic, inventive, fast all at the same time, a real inspiration.

And anyway, what's wrong with speed? Coltrane played fast, so did Cecil Taylor. Bach is fast, Philip Glass is fast. Bad Brains were fast and totally accurate. Lou Reed was once billed in The Velvets as 'the world's fastest guitarist'. When I heard Coltrane it was (on one level, anyway) more guitar heroics to me — only he did it with a saxophone. Absorbing punk rock did not negate having guitar heroes. I remember Henry Kaiser saying how Richard Thompson is cool because he can play sloppy or dead-on precise, and someone like Steve Morse of The Dixie Dregs could only play impressive stuff, which made him less of a guitar player. That really resonated with me. I always found energy and mistakes interesting. I watched a Janis Joplin clip on MTV with my groupmates in Shattered Glass and they were laughing at her guitarist (either Sam Andrew or James Gurley) who was out of tune and flailing away; I was totally into it. That was just as valid as Clapton or Van Halen, not more, not less.

Anyway, once David Lee Roth left Van Halen I lost interest. By that point I was out of the covers group, playing punk rock, listening to Glenn Branca, Steve Reich and Brian Eno; being able to play 'Eruption' was probably more of a liability that an asset. It was a joke. But I never forgot it.

Alan Licht is a US musician, composer and writer

LYDIA LUNCH ON THE INDUSTRIAL OPERA OF A
NEW YORK RACE RIOT AND THE MUSIC THAT
SOUNDTRACKED IT

1967

Blood buckets down the undulating walls. Invisible fists
rage with superhuman strength and hammer the door. The
ancient wood frame buckles, crumples and heaves. The
empty nursery reverberates with the mournful howl of a
pitiful infant, who cannot be located. I'm sitting cross-legged
on the floor, clutching my throat, trembling. Dry mouthed.
Unable to breathe. *The Haunting Of Hill House* is the most
terrifying movie I've ever seen. I'm eight years old.

A suffocating humidity saturates the night air. Static
electricity vibrates the hair follicles. The low buzzing hum of
the black and white Motorola is swallowed up in the wheezing
yelp of a stray dog, which bellows like a town crier somewhere
in someone's backyard. His harried yapping immediately
mimicked and amplified by every mutt in the neighborhood
in a round robin of barks and howls. A desperate warning cry,
which signals the coming maelstrom.

The atmosphere stiffens. The dogs retreat. Time bends.
In a sudden explosion of white noise, hundreds of frenzied
voices come shrieking out of nowhere. As if all hell's fury,
in a sudden expulsion from middle earth, materialises,
compounding my terror.

Men, women and their children who have been hoisted
upon the backs of older brothers, all shouting slogans in a
demonic gospeled fervour. Equal work! Equal pay! We're
Black and Proud and here to stay! Black Power!

The riots of 1967 have detoured down Clifford Avenue,
and are stampeding directly in front of my house in
Rochester, New York. Hammers, baseball bats, pipes and
bricks, all employed in the demolition of cars, windows,
storefronts. A hideous industrial opera of unbearable din.
My father chain smokes and paces, unleashing a litany of
curses. He punches the air in his best Marlon Brando as his

station wagon crumbles under the endless battery of physical abuse. The ambulance and fire trucks barrel in, splitting the angry throng in two, their sirens a deafening symphony which exaggerate the cacophony. Police helicopters circle the periphery. Giant mechanical insects whose diabolical hum blankets the shrill.

My fear is drowned in sound but reborn as joy in flames. The family car is set on fire. I start to laugh. Manically. To dance. To sing. *'Come on baby LIGHT my FIRE. Try to set the night on FIRE!!!!'*. My father assumes I've lost my mind, and against my insistent protest sends me to my room.

I skulk upstairs dejected, 'kind of a drag' mumbled under my breath. A noisy rebellion of violence, clanging, pounding, exciting. And I'm locked out! I can't really comprehend what's happening, but it feels right. I'm no longer frightened, I'm charged up. Zoning in to the collective urgency. The passion. Determination. I head to the attic, my hidden retreat. Turn on the radio. Top 40 in 1967 was insane. 'White Rabbit', 'Seven Rooms Of Gloom', 'Funky Broadway', 'The Hunter Gets Captured By The Game', 'Are You Experienced?'. Back to back. I had no idea what any of these songs were referencing. What they really meant. How subversive they really were.

I used the radio to disappear. Escape from my family. Enter another dimension. Melt inside a psychedelic sound stage which cascaded out through the airwaves filling my already fractured psyche with a throbbing, slinky, funkified soul music, where soaring rhythms and strangled guitars took me out of myself and gave me goose bumps. James Brown's *'I wake up... in a cold sweat'* stimulated me in ways I could only express by shaking my ass, flapping my arms and stomping my feet. Jimmy Lee Johnson, the seven year old black boy next door, 'skinny legs and all', had the entire JB 'drop to one knee, use the sweatshirt as a cape' routine down pat. It's the first time anyone flirted with me. I was amazed by his mimicry. His fluidity. His tiny body gliding through the air with so much passion and control. He really knew how to shake a tail feather. He must have caught JB on *The Ed Sullivan Show*. Everybody was glued to the tube on Sunday nights. The Rolling Stones doing 'Let's Spend The

Night Together', The Animals, George Carlin all penetrated my unformed psyche, courtesy of Mr Sullivan. Even the infamous Doors controversy where Morrison refused to change *'Girl we couldn't get much higher'* and subsequently got banned from future appearances struck a raw nerve in my adolescent consciousness.

Music is the connective tissue between protest, rebellion, violence, sexual awareness and community. Just the way it is. The Summer of Love. What a bold faced lie! Reagan was elected Governor of California. Lyndon B Johnson increased troop presence in Vietnam, ignoring the massive demonstrations, which rocked the nightly news. 70,000 strong in New York alone. Race riots stormed through Cleveland, Detroit, Watts, Birmingham, Alabama, Rochester, New York and hundreds of other US cities inflaming tensions. Muhammad Ali was stripped of his World Heavyweight Championship title for refusing the draft. Carl Wilson of The Beach Boys wouldn't go to war either and got tied up in a five year legal battle, which he eventually won. The Boston Strangler was sentenced to life in prison and escaped from the institution he was held in.

Bread was 22 cents a loaf, a gallon of gas was 28 cents and the inner city ghetto which I called home was brimming with hard working people with attitude and conviction, whose lust for life couldn't be beaten out of them by piss-poor housing conditions, lousy pay, the police or politicians. They taught me to fight for what I believed in, take pride in what I did, never give up, keep the faith and when hoping for a better tomorrow isn't enough, to turn up the music and dance them damn blues away.

Well, you can take the wigger out of the ghetto, but you can't take the ghetto out of the wigger. After all, 'The World Is A Ghetto'. And even though I'll never forget my roots, I refused to allow them to strangle me by the ankles because even if I had to 'beg borrow and steal', this 'Lightning's Girl' was going to be sure she was 'Making Every Minute Count'. Just like the radio taught me.

1967 helped define who I was to become. I may have been too young to fully grasp the political implications of the time, but it started a fire in my belly that burns as bright today as it ever did. The National Organisation of Women was officially incorporated in 67. Grace Slick and Janis Joplin both threw down at the Monterey Pop festival. Shirley Temple ran for congress. I was just a tiny terror screaming my bloody head off to 'Funky Broadway', already plotting my big city escape.

Lydia Lunch is a US musician, writer and spoken word performer

It was the mid-1970s, and I was becoming increasingly fascinated by noise. I was a chubby schoolboy at Wath Grammar School, South Yorkshire (in the background, a young William Hague was poring over his textbooks), and all my mates were into soul music or progressive rock, with the exception of Steve Bucknell, who loved the blues, and Dave Sunderland, who loved piano jazz, particularly Oscar Peterson. Sometimes I would go up to his house and watch in wonder as he set up a huge spaghetti of wires and coat hangers so that he could pick up Voice Of America in his back room. Above the hiss, you could just hear Oscar. Oddly, I liked the hiss best; or rather, the combination of hiss and Oscar.

Speaking of Oscar, I was playing drums in a group called Oscar The Frog. We were ostensibly folk rock, and practised in the church hall, doing Fairport Convention and Mr Fox numbers. The bit I liked best, though, was the end of the rehearsal. Steve Sutcliffe, the violinist, would say in a sonorous voice amplified by the church hall's high walls and ceilings, 'Let's progress!', and the five of us would make delicious, delirious noise until the caretaker came in and said, 'Right, that's enough: it's just a row, now', and chuck us out.

But folk rock wasn't quite enough for my soul, and before our first gig — at a church jumble sale — I tried to persuade the lads that we should do a ten minute 'Progression' rather than the jigs, reels and version of 'Matty Groves' we had planned. But I couldn't convince them: we played our ten minutes and then the curtains shut. No applause, no reaction. At the same time, I was getting my real musical education from John Peel's radio show. I remember Soft Machine, Keith Tippett, Wild Man Fischer and, most wonderfully of all, Captain Beefheart. My Uncle Charlie told me that a beefheart was a cabbage, and I only half believed him. Steve Bucknell dismissed Beefheart as a blues shouter, not half as good as the dead people he liked, and the rest of Oscar The Frog dismissed my idea that we should do a medley of 'Sir Patrick Spens' and 'Moonlight On Vermont'.

My 15th birthday was approaching, and for my Big Present from my mam and dad I wanted the mighty Captain's *Lick My Decals Off, Baby*. Under the influence of John Peel, Monty Python and a vague feeling of adolescent rebellion, I set up Wath Grammar School Bizarre Club and began to work on my Theory of Accidental Climaxes, which isn't as onanistic as it might sound. The Bizarre Club was an attempt to do odd dadaistic things in a grammar school context. The Theory of Accidental Climaxes formed part of my noise discovery. I noticed that when people were talking in the classroom, there was a general low level hum, then suddenly a lot of people would talk at once, and then the low hum would return. Chair-scrapings, dropped pencils and banging doors added to the mix. I started notating the Accidental Climaxes when I should have been writing about Political History.

On Sundays I went to my Auntie and Uncle Charlie's house for tea, and we would sit and watch TV eating cold beef sandwiches until the appointed hour, when the TV would go off, the vast radiogramme would be switched on, and we would have to listen to *Sing Something Simple* with The Adams Singers, and Jack Emblow on the accordion. This was almost too much to bear. As the opening lines *'Sing something simple, as cares go by...'* wafted across the dark room, my brain began to turn to sludge and I'd feel as if I'd been awake for three weeks. Then I began to notice something: you could pick out whole universes of sound within The Adams Singers' treacly harmonies! Somehow John Peel, Soft Machine and Captain Beefheart were educating my ears. Uncle Charlie had worked down the pit for 40 years and his chest was in a terrible state; as he breathed, it sounded like people walking on gravel. The breathing, and Auntie's Hoover, and the ice cream van outside, and the kids on the street playing football, mixed with The Adams Singers into something extraordinary. But the lads from Oscar The Frog wouldn't have any of this: they thought I was getting too daft for my own good.

As my birthday approached, I told my parents what I wanted. They looked worried. 'Are you still working hard for your 'O' Levels?' they asked; I assured them I was. My dad said that I should buy the record for myself, but I said he should buy it, because it wouldn't feel like a present if I did. He agreed, and we went to Neal's Music Shop up the Arcade in Barnsley. My dad had decided that if he went up to the assistant and said, 'Lick my decals off, baby', it might cause some kind of incident that would end up being reported in *The Barnsley Chronicle,* so he wrote it on a piece of paper and passed it to the assistant. She read it, blushed, and sent for Mr Neal himself. It was a kind of Accidental Climax all on its own. Mr Neal and my dad discussed things for a bit, and it was eventually settled amicably. My dad didn't say anything all the way home. Next day I received *Lick My Decals Off, Baby* giftwrapped with a label that read 'love from Mum and Dad'.

After my dad had gone to work, I just had time to listen to a couple of tracks before I went to school. A strange thing happened in the English lesson. Mr Manchester broke off talking about *Macbeth* and picked up the album. I thought he was going to confiscate it, but he wasn't that kind of teacher. 'My wife's supposed to be getting me this for my birthday,' he said. 'I hope it's as good as *Trout Mask Replica.'*

It was a time of epiphanies, and there was more to come. That Sunday, I took the album to Auntie and Uncle Charlie's. After the beef sandwiches, *Sing Something Simple* began, and I put *Lick My Decals Off, Baby* on. Uncle Charlie was in his chair, his breath rattling. Auntie was washing up in the kitchen, and the pots rattled shrilly. You could only do one thing at once on the radiogramme, so I couldn't, as first planned, play Beefheart under The Adams Singers. Instead I switched rapidly between them: for a couple of wonderful, life affirming minutes we had a snatch of Beefheart and a line of Cliff Adams, clashing, crashing, melting together and forcing each other apart. Uncle Charlie had been nodding off, but now he was fully awake. 'Is there something up with the bloody wireless?' he said loudly. I smiled. Across the village, Dave Sunderland was listening to Oscar Peterson; in the next village, the other members of Oscar The Frog were putting together a version of Fairport Convention's 'Sloth'. At 34 North Street, my Auntie was shouting, Uncle Charlie was gasping for breath, and I was somewhere between *Sing*

Something Simple and Captain Beefheart in a place I think they call Heaven.

Ian MacMillan is a UK poet and broadcaster

It was early August 1985, and Boris Grebnschikov was telling
me in fluent, Brit-accented English that he'd wanted to be a
rock star from the time he was 12, 'because there was no place
in society for someone like me'. We were sitting in the kitchen
of his communal apartment in central Leningrad, which was
bohemian bordering on the squalid.

Pre-Gorbachev, but at the beginning of the collapse of
the Soviet Union, Boris wore his hair long and shaggy with
a headband. In his early thirties, he was the leading light of
the Soviet rock underground, or unofficial scene. That meant
he didn't produce records, tour or appear locally in formal
concerts, couldn't buy equipment through the government-
sanctioned Musicians Union, but neither did he have to
win its approval for his songs, or depend upon its bookings
for his career.

Officially, Boris had no career: he had an undemanding,
low-level, part-time day job. He wasn't working as an engineer;
the profession for which he'd trained. Nonetheless, his music
was widely known.

'I make my albums on tape,' he explained. 'I give the
tapes to my friends, and they are duplicated on tape, and
passed on, all over the country. I know this because I got
letters from fans. Perhaps there is only one person in a town
who writes to me, but letters come from everywhere in the
Soviet Union.'

He was proud of his reputation, and even prouder of
the four-track tapes he played for me on a battered reel-to-
reel machine, which he slapped every time one of the stereo
channels went out. On one tape he'd cannibalised early 70s
Kinks songs for Dave Davies's lead lines. He'd concocted his
own version of *Sgt Pepper's*, lifting George Martin's chorus
of French horns, changing the melodies but retaining the
phrasings. He was fascinated by Celtic lore, believing there
was a link between early Anglo-Saxon and early Slavic
peoples, and for his research had studied *Lord Of The Rings*,

among other fables. Considering himself a spiritual person in a culture where 'people would deny there's a sun even if they're standing in the sunshine', Boris listened avidly to The Incredible String Band and UB40. He apologised for never having gotten into The Clash. 'In theory, I liked them but I couldn't enjoy listening to them.'

Another tape he played me contained an improvised electronic version of The Doors' 'The End', with orgasmic wailing by gypsy vocalist Valentina Ponomareva, who had long participated in Leningrad's undergound rock and avant garde jazz culture, but had recently accepted official status. A few days later, I saw Ponomareva on Soviet television, daubed with make-up, singing an overwrought ballad and dancing in a tutu.

Boris and his immediate family shared their apartment with about half a dozen other people, who came and went through his 'office', an unassigned room he'd appropriated, as though it was everyone's den. Did he get along with all his commune mates? 'Well... The young man who just looked in on us, for instance,' he said by way of reply, and referring to a recent visitor, 'he was lately released from prison, where he served four years for burglary. Sometimes I think the KGB has put him in this apartment to keep them informed of what I'm doing. He's very curious, wants to know everything, asks a lot of questions.' When I leave Boris's apartment to catch the subway before it closes down for the night, a door on the fourth floor landing opens a crack, and the pale young man's face is illuminated by the bulb behind him. He glances at me, shuts the door. He hovers about during the rest of my meeting with Boris.

'The government is aware of all my activity.' Boris tells me. 'I'm not against the government; I'm very much for the government. I do not take any money from it; I'm allowed to do what I want to do. Of course they could stop me whenever they want to, but why should they bother? I'm only a musician. I think I'm working under the best of conditions.' In 1988, Boris would move to America and sign a brief, star-crossed deal with CBS. But at the time we met, he still imagined that rock stars in the US must find wealth and fame distracting.

It was possible he was being ironic, but he seemed truly dedicated, without pretence or urgency or apparent bitterness.

I'd missed seeing Boris perform with his eclectic group Aquarium. They held open rehearsals at a factory hall, and gave infrequently mounted performances, promoted solely by word of mouth, in a loft inhabited by the avant garde Zero artists group (situated directly across the street from the KGB's Leningrad headquarters). But on my last night in the Soviet Union, a Sunday, I was invited to a clandestine house concert in an apartment building at the end of a metro line. I wasn't given the address; instead I was picked up at the station by Sergey Kuryokhin, the pianist, composer and leader of Popular Mechanics who died in 1996, and who was always humming and whistling like he had a Casio implant in his head. With him was Boris's pale young neighbour.

Boris sat on the floor of a living room lit by candles, wearing a harmonica rack but no shirt, his acoustic guitar in his lap. The audience consisted of 18 men and women, including two American students who were celebrating their wedding and had brought a couple of bottles of vodka. Boris mostly strummed rhythm, and sang his original lyrics in a soft but impassioned voice, reminiscent of Bob Dylan, if not Woody Guthrie. Boris himself might have cited the Soviet actor-singer-songwriter Vladimir Vysotski, whose grave, on the anniversary of his death, is mobbed like Presley's Graceland mansion.

After more than an hour, Boris sang The Grateful Dead's 'Uncle John's Band' and a Buffalo Springfield song, in honour of the Americans; then Sergey sat at the piano and, with Boris, played a simple blues. One of the Americans improvised a lyric. I didn't take notes, and it's now long forgotten, but it was supposed to be funny, wry, sad, yet a protest, meant to acknowledge we'd all known troubles, but weren't about to complain that life or politics are killers. They are of course, everywhere.

Howard Mandel is president of the American Jazz Journalists Association

Between 1969 and 1975 I was infatuated with the music of the
quintessential American composer Charles Edward Ives —
and once I dreamed that he actually kissed me. It was a rough,
manly kiss, planted firmly in the centre of my forehead. Of
all the erogenous zones available to him, this was the least of
them. I accepted it for what it was: a benediction.

It was appropriate that I receive his blessing. After all, I'd
been listening to his music exclusively for the best part of half
a decade. I'd read everything about and by him that was in the
public domain. I was, without a shadow of doubt, his Number
One Fan. And in one of my various other Charles Ives dreams
I'd conjured up a New England colonial-style clapboard edifice
called the Ives Hotel, situated in Stockbridge, MA, whose
residents included Henry Cowell and Henry Cow, Anthony
Braxton, Karlheinz Stockhausen, John Cage, Harry Partch,
Henry Brant, Frank Zappa, Peter Maxwell Davies, Christian
Wolff, Captain Beefheart and a host of other composer/
performers in whose music I detected (often mistakenly) an
Ivesian element. I imagined them relaxing on the porch of an
evening, sipping iced tea in the deepening twilight and trading
musical anecdotes, while small-town America dreamed itself
anew. I was the manager of the hotel, in whom everyone
confided. I knew absolutely everything.

My interest in Ives was obsessive. While working at
bookshop, tax office, building site, warehouse, etc, his music
so fully occupied my mind it left little room for thought. I
was a drudge employee, doing no more and more often
less than the job required, and doing it without flair or
imagination. But without the engrossing distractions of
Ives's music, I probably wouldn't have been able to hold
down a job at all. During the evenings, in a succession of
cramped and shabby bedsits, I crouched over my typewriter,
and while Ives LPs spun on the turntable I two-fingeredly
pecked out notes, copious notes. By 1974 I had more than a
thousand pages of them.

What did they consist of? Poetic doodles, mostly.
Sometimes a single word sat centre page, a word so
powerful and enigmatic that it banished lesser words from
its presence. Other pages were heavily embellished, then
embellished again, crammed to the margins with tiny,
semi-comprehensible scribbles that defied translation
into typescript. Eventually, a friend took pity on me and
suggested that I write a critical work about Ives, or at least
research him properly. He helped me to track down and
complete the necessary forms. Funds were to be sought from
a cultural foundation. Another friend of mine persuaded a
friend of his, a musicologist, to provide technical assistance.
I went along with the plan only because it legitimised my
obsession.

The Ives LPs were stacked beside the turntable. All other
LPs had been banished to the wardrobe and saw the light
of day only when visitors requested music that wasn't by
Charles Ives. Those were the kind of visitors I didn't much
care for. Frankly, I found it inconceivable that someone
might prefer to hear something other than the evocative and
exultant *Three Places In New England*, the avant garde horse
opera soundtrack that is *Charlie Rutlage*, the ear-bending,
experimentally tripartite *Tone Roads*, the creative tumult and
rugged expressiveness of the *Robert Browning Overture* and
Piano Sonata No 1, the dazzling redistributions of material
in *An Old Song Deranged*, the serene transcendentalism that
informs *The Unanswered Question* and the hard-won (all
the more satisfying) resolution of *String Quartet No 2*. Ives
had, to my way of thinking, something for everyone, though
presumably not everyone agreed.

When I visited friends I always took three or four
Ives LPs with me, and always managed to slip one onto
the turntable while a Strawbs LP was being resleeved and
something by Jefferson Airplane or Miles Davis was being
selected. In retrospect, I can see that people were remarkably
tolerant of my idiosyncrasies, but at the time I thought I was
doing them a huge favour. After all, my records were so much
more interesting than theirs! They even took it quite well
when I provided disparaging running commentaries on the

music of their favourite groups. I remember telling a staunch Zappaphile that the tricky time signatures on *Hot Rats* (and *Uncle Meat*, too!) came straight out of the Presto movement of Ives's chronically undervalued *Piano Trio*, and that the other good bits of Zappa's music had been cribbed from Edgard Varèse. Had I not been deaf to everything but my own wayward opinions, I suspect that I would have heard the sound of grinding teeth.

What was important about Charles Ives, something that I tried to communicate to anyone who was prepared to listen, was that his can-do experimentalism kick-started 20th century American music. His compositions made use of tone rows, noise, microtonality, etc. But what I liked about him most was his exuberance. He was a complicated individual, full of the most amazing contradictions, and these fed directly into his music. That's why much of it is rough hewn and seemingly unfinished. Unlike the prissy, anal perfectionism typical of the music of his day, Ives's compositions were untidy, unruly and gloriously imperfect. This wasn't a failing of some kind, as Elliott Carter thought, but a bold aesthetic ploy. Should one always try to reconcile elements, or filter out materials that clash? Ives obviously thought not. Snatches of ragtime, mawkishly sentimental parlour ballads, hymn tunes, Abolitionist songs and country band marches were given equal standing with the loftier elements of composition. High-minded sentiments rubbed shoulders with low skits and musical jokes. It was a serious music that wasn't afraid to laugh at itself. 'I want to be at least as alive as the vulgar,' declared the poet Frank O'Hara, a sentiment with which I suspect Charles Ives would have agreed.

What became of my grand obsession? It ran its course. I lost a job and didn't get round to applying for another. I bathed less often than was necessary. I took to sleeping during the day and listening to music and writing all night. Then, in 1975, I published a book that didn't make reference to Charles Ives; not a single mention. I'd moved on almost without realising it. No prospect of further manly kisses from Ives, no more vivid New England dreams. His LPs became increasingly neglected. They acquired a fine layer of dust. Eventually they went into the wardrobe and others came out to play.

Brian Marley is a UK writer and photographer

BARRY MILES ON EXPERIENCING THE BEATLES'
GROUP MIND AND STUDIO SMARTS FIRSTHAND

In the summer of 1951, I heard 'How High The Moon' by Les
Paul and Mary Ford on the radio. I didn't know the title or
artist, but my aunt took me to the local Currys — records were
mostly sold through electrical goods shops back then — to
try and find it. When asked what the record sounded like, I
apparently told the assistant that it was like rainbow bubbles
floating over a wall in the sunlight. I was just eight years old.
That record turned me on to music.

All through art school and my early days living in a
communal flat in Notting Hill in West London I sat around
with friends listening to jazz: cascades of piano notes from
Cecil Taylor, birdsong from Eric Dolphy, air sculpture by
John Coltrane, honks and squeaks by Albert Ayler. When
a new release entered the pad we would sit in the living
room, smoke something to open our ears, and play it at least
three times before anyone would dare venture an opinion.
Although I had adored 50s doowop and artists like Chuck
Berry, Fats Domino and Little Richard, 60s pop music passed
me by until the summer of 1965, when I met The Beatles.

That year I cofounded Indica Books and Gallery. One of
my partners, Peter Asher, still lived at his parents' home, as
did his sister Jane and her boyfriend Paul McCartney. The
Asher household on Wimpole Street was only five minutes
walk from where I lived and I used the Ashers' basement
to assemble the stock for the bookshop while we looked for
premises. I got to know Paul McCartney pretty well; we went
to concerts and plays together as well as nightclubs. That
October he invited me to a Beatles recording session, the
first of many.

The fans waiting outside Abbey Road did not come
as a surprise; there were always a dozen or so outside the
Asher house. It was the contrast that was so extraordinary.
Outside were the trappings of fame with girls thrusting
presents into their hands; inside Studio Two represented
total musical professionalism.

These days people are familiar with recording studios from videos and films, but then it was unknown territory. Abbey Road was a mixture of the BBC and *Flash Gordon*: men in brown labcoats holding clipboards peered at enormous dials. The equipment was huge and, though I didn't know it then, obsolete. EMI built their own equipment and it was designed to last: enormous semi-circular VU meters and doorknob size pan-pots to position the stereo image; it all looked as if it came from the bridge of a battle cruiser. To listen to a playback was a complex business. A tape op would have to unplug dozens of patch cords and reposition them, like in a primitive telephone exchange.

They were recording a new McCartney song, 'I'm Looking Through You', which eventually appeared on *Rubber Soul*. He and Jane had been having some difficulties because she had chosen to play a season with the Bristol Old Vic theatre company instead of staying in town with him. This song was the result of their arguments. The session began with a band meeting with George Martin to discuss the arrangement. Paul seemed to have a pretty good idea how the song should go but as I saw from later sessions, The Beatles operated as a democracy and each Beatle had his say about the treatment of a song and what contribution he could bring to it. The first thing that astonished me was that they didn't just set up and play as if they were in a theatre, they used the studio like an instrument, treating each song separately with an arrangement to suit its musical needs: a sitar, a string quartet, sound effects.

For 'I'm Looking Through You' the instrumentation was Ringo on handclaps and maracas, George Martin on organ, Paul playing a closely miked acoustic guitar, and George Harrison on electric. It took some time to get the separation the engineers needed and to decide on the arrangement; who came in when.

The mic positioning was all important to the sound, achieving a clarity and separation that I quickly realised was only possible in a multitrack studio, albeit a four-track one. To an outsider like me it all seemed chaotic with people playing and talking over each other. Then there was a countdown and they began to play; perfectly in tune, musically as well as with each other.

They were consummate players. The hundreds of hours of performing together in Hamburg and at the Cavern in Liverpool meant they knew instinctively what each was about to do: the 'group mind'. They stopped before the end but already the song seemed to me to be almost there. They explained some of the technical details to me: for instance, they had the vocal microphone set slightly high so they had to stretch their necks to sing instead of looking down and constricting their air passages. There were so many ways this song could have been treated, but they knew almost at once how to approach it and by the end of the session had what sounded to me like a perfect take, marred only by an over-ambitious electric solo by George which could have been overdubbed anew. They had transformed a few notes on the back of a shirt packet into a work of art. (In fact they were not satisfied and rerecorded the song from scratch a few days later.)

It really was a revelation to me. I went out and bought records by The Beatles and Stones, Dylan and the Motown acts that McCartney told me about. From then on I bored my friends with endless discussions about the emergence of a new art form; how pop music — as it was then called — was the vehicle for musical experimentation; about the possibilities of the studio as an instrument; and how The Beatles were leading a musical revolution. Friends accepted my enthusiasm with amused tolerance, but The Beatles themselves were more receptive, and I had long talks with McCartney about the subject. We listened a lot to John Cage, Luciano Berio, Stockhausen, Albert Ayler, as well as The Beach Boys, R&B and an IBM 7000 computer singing 'Daisy Daisy'. His attitude to music convinced me that pop was the future. In a conversation I recorded in 1966, McCartney said: 'With any kind of thing, my aim seems to be to distort it. Distort it from what we know it as, even with music, with visual things. But the aim is to change it from what it is to see what it could be. To see the potential in it all. The point is to take a note and wreck the note and see in that note what else there is in it that a simple act like distorting it has caused.' To me this was pop music taking over where Ayler, Dolphy and Coltrane left off. It was the rainbow bubbles all over again; it was a revelation.

Barry Miles is a UK author

Citizens of future civilisations who want to portray us as a backward and boneheaded lot will have plenty of examples to choose from. They could cite the fact that ten per cent of our global population hogs 85 per cent of global wealth. Or they could look at our attitude to amplification.

Musicians in our culture often have a weirdly sadistic, militaristic attitude to volume; they aspire to shock and awe, to full spectrum dominance. In *Do You Love Me Like I Love You*, the film Iain Forsyth and Jane Pollard made to accompany some reissues of Nick Cave albums, one of the talking heads recalls, with apparent admiration, how Cave, on being told his live performance is great, invariably responds, 'Yes, but was it loud enough?'

When My Bloody Valentine reformed in 2008, their London Roundhouse performances hit 119 decibels, dislodging dust and plaster high in the building. MBV's Kevin Shields, a man reputed in the 1980s to have had hearing so sharp he could detect a phone ringing in an office a quarter of a mile away, now hears a permanent telephone ringing in his head. 'I got tinnitus falling asleep listening to mixes of *Loveless*,' Shields would later announce.

Being pounded into submission by looming black amplifier cabinets has been the backdrop to most of my concertgoing life, but when I think about the moments when I've been truly mesmerised by live music, they've often been subversively quiet ones — gestures of rebellion, perhaps, against mainstream rock's dark religion of force, its ego-driven need to damage the human body by going beyond what our frail ears are designed to bear.

The first rock show I remember actually damaging my hearing (one ear didn't work properly for days afterwards) was XTC at Edinburgh's Odeon Cinema in 1981. That same year, I had my first taste of the seductive qualities of quiet music in the form of an outdoor festival of John Cage music in Rome. In a courtyard lit by burning torches, two prepared pianos, unamplified, traded the light, strange, beautiful percussive cascades of his 1945 piece *Daughters Of The Lonesome Isle*. If rock's thunder of drums, bass and guitars represented what Susan Sontag called 'aggressive normality', these modified pianos were the sound of a gentle, intriguing deviance.

The difference was clear physiologically. Instead of making me tamp down tensely for some kind of assault or endurance test, Cage's music made my body relax and open up. The threshold of my aural sensitivity lowered, and I began to hear more and more. Not just the music, but the ambient sounds in the courtyard, the crackling of the torches under the eaves, the distant sound of a police siren. The act of listening became delightful. As in Aesop's fable 'The Wind And The Sun', warmth was able to do what storm wind couldn't.

When I became a performer myself, I discovered how hard it is to achieve effective quietness on stage. All sorts of things militate against it: sound engineers, drummers, air conditioning systems, vocal Saturday night crowds, traffic, alcohol, indifference. But I also discovered that, when there's a basic attitude of trust and respect between a performer and an audience, quietness can be more powerful than volume. Something extraordinary happens when you reach a certain level of quietness — there's a sudden intensity in the room, a direct sensual bond with the audience. The spaces between the notes begin to matter more, allowing a whole new sense of colour and form to emerge in the music. The Japanese call it ma: negative space, the structural use of emptiness.

Some years ago I was on tour in Ohio and stopped at Oberlin College. A student group called The Gongs happened to be playing that night, and I entered a darkened classroom to join a tiny audience ranged around four musicians seated in a stage area defined by rugs, boxes and old window frames. Mysterious steel gongs hung from the ceiling. Two members of the group played microtonal lutes, a third created drones on a detuned harmonium, while lanky Peter Blasser, the group's leader, tweaked Harry Partch-like notes from an absurdly long electric slide instrument shaped from driftwood. I found The Gongs' music completely mesmerising, and signed the group to my label American Patchwork. The following year, touring the US with them,

I discovered that the quiet intensity of that Oberlin show couldn't be recreated in rock clubs. People just talked through their set.

The music I love most right now is *Ombrophilia*, the debut album by my friend Tomoko Sauvage, issued by the Seattle label and/OAR. Ombrophilia means 'an abnormal love of rain'. Tomoko uses wooden cooking spoons to strike and stir Chinese porcelain rice bowls filled with water. The wobbly, chiming vessels turn tuned water into a sort of natural synthesizer, complete with organic forms of envelope, modulation, pitchbend and decay. Tomoko captures the gloopy, ringing sonorities with subaquatic mic probes, then feeds the result through digital processing. Track titles like 'Amniotic Life' reveal that she's drawn inspiration from the fluid sounds of her recent pregnancy — her own internal 'waters' and the new life moving within them.

This is super-quiet music, filled with something sweeter and sexier than rock's morbid, normative love of pain. When Tomoko plays it live, water dripping from a pierced polythene bag hung from the ceiling not only adds a kind of random percussion, but scatters reflections off the lit water surface across the walls and ceiling. The result is soothing and sensual, like a long hot bath. I could soak in it forever.

Momus, aka Nicholas Currie, is a Scottish singer, musician and writer

ALEX NEILSON ON THE NOCTURNAL SOLITUDE
EVOKED BY FRANK SINATRA'S SADDEST SONGS

'*Each place I go*
Only the lonely know,
Some little small cafe.
The songs I know
Only the lonely know,
Each melody recalls a love that used to be'

So starts an album whose mood, like the colour of its cover, is
as black as any star-abandoned night. An album that speaks
with such penetrating poetry about certain melancholic
predicaments you might find yourself in at the wrong side of
4am. An album that the artist's son described as 'the greatest
blues album ever made', which certainly explains that
yearning soul sickness equally as eloquently as any of those
spooked old Skip James recordings. The album is *Only The
Lonely* by Francis Albert Sinatra.

Like the middle aged man who has buckled beneath the
weight of the world and turned to the church for cold consola-
tion, I was at a real creative crossroads when this album was
first played to me, and ready to disregard the old routes I had
been pursuing. I was in the process of resensitising myself to
possibilities previously dismissed for fear of betraying some
very narrow sense of purity of expression. I gained a lot of
courage from the good book (Graham Robb's 2001 biography
of Arthur Rimbaud), which indicated that one could pursue
some vast, unnameable creative elixir with furious dedication
but then eventually step away from the brink before it forever
consigned you to a life of alienation and self-obstruction. In
embracing an artist as ubiquitous and sentimental as Frank
Sinatra, whole glittering vistas of creative possibility revealed
themselves to me.

I know there is a certain stigma to Sinatra among young,
hip, Facebook-slurping types (generation-i). He will never
have the kind of arthouse credibility of, say, Scott Walker
(an artist whom my brother once glibly described as 'Sartre

meets Sinatra'), and that is, in part, understandable. Sinatra never wrote a song based on an Ingmar Bergman film or retreated from pop stardom to make music with the kind of sledgehammer grandeur of *Tilt* or *Climate Of Hunter*. But way back in the late 1950s/early 60s, he did record a clutch of albums that are saturated in such desperate, nocturnal angst, they make Walker sound like Paolo Nutini's bummer uncle, of which *Only The Lonely* is his crowning glory.

Recorded in 1958, just a year after *A Swinging Affair* and *Come Fly With Me*, *Only The Lonely* is the antithesis of the kind of pop candyfloss for which Sinatra is better remembered. *Only The Lonely* has about as much swing as Nick Griffin absent-mindedly whistling 'Hitler Has Only Got One Ball' at a BNP rally in a Little Chef on Coventry 's outer ring road. The album contains subtle, near-subliminal orchestrations by Nelson Riddle which provide the perfect black scaffolding for Sinatra's Scotch-rich voice to fill the speaker space like cigar smoke.

Take the closing track on side one, 'Goodbye'. A high, lonesome oboe ushers in the opening motif, which morphs into a cello, then sinks into a double bass. Then a pregnant pause that hangs like an existential question mark over the song, before that famous, sensuous voice intones:

> '*I'll never forget you* [long pause]
> *I'll neevvvver forrrget yooouu* [longer pause]
> *I'll never forget how we promised one day*
> *To love one another forever that way.*
> *We said we'd never say* [long, dramatic pause]
> *Goooooodbyyyyyeeeee*
> [a flood of kettle drums and strings]
> *But that was long agoooooooooo*
> *Now you've forgotten, I know*'

The thing that is most difficult to convey when simply reciting the lyrics is the drama of Sinatra's phrasing along with the directness of the poetry, which combine to invest the music with such gravity. The singer can effortlessly evoke a scene as simple and universal as two lovers promenading along a willow-flanked river, not holding hands but brushing arms as they drink in each other's presence, then turn it on a sixpence with those treacherous modifiers, *'but'* or *'except'*. Sinatra will zone in on a detail traditionally associated with beauty and then use it to trigger some pathetic situation from his/her/your/my past. Every sunset recalls an absent love. Every flower the scent of her hair. Behind every hello, a heartache.

It's also important to try to imagine American life in the 1950s/early 60s. A nation that hit the ground running while the old guard of Europe struggled to its feet after the Second World War. A nation that was the richest and most technologically advanced that the world had ever known. But there is a palpable melancholy at the heart of the music, art and literature of the time. Artists like JD Salinger, Miles Davis, Jack Kerouac and Edward Hopper all attest to a big city loneliness, addressing themes like ageing, alienation, betrayal, unrequited love — a tapestry of black shades that all the gaudy glitz in the world cannot refract light from. In *Only The Lonely*, Sinatra surveys this demi-monde with an unflinching eye, unafraid to wear his heart on his sleeve for the city pigeons to peck at. When he sings lines like *'So, drink up all you people/Order anything you see/And have fun, you happy people/The drink and the laugh's on me/'Scuse me, while I disappear'* it feels loaded with the bathos of one who can see beyond the dollar bill-thin veneer of Manhattan's garrulous, Martini-quaffing classes. Of one who has survived every kind of night. Of one who possesses greater virtues and still greater failings than most men.

Sinatra was also embroiled in a complex nexus of relationships at the time of the recording, courting some of the most celebrated women in the world: Judy Garland, Kim Novak and Lauren Bacall. But despite this embarrassment of 'rich bitches', it seems Sinatra had never got over that great, ruinous love, Ava 'Hurricane' Gardner. In the early 50s his voice was cracking under the stress of a dwindling career and shovelfuls of prescription medication, and he is rumoured to have made a number of suicide attempts. By the mid-late 50s Sinatra's voice had matured into that sonorous, oak-strength quality you can hear on *Only The Lonely*. It's as if he used the vocal imperfections and the tempestuous situations of his recent past in his performances as a row of emotional black holes, reporting back from their precipices. Indeed, for pure emotional evisceration I would put *Only The Lonely* on a par with Van Morrison's *Astral Weeks*, John Coltrane's *Olatunji Concert* and John Dowland's 'Lachrimae'.

Sinatra's music, at its best, is the stuff of high drama. His other albums around that time that touch upon similar degrees of elevated melancholia are *In The Wee Small Hours Of The Morning*, *No One Cares* and *Point Of No Return*, but I've heard it said that there is a detectable, slow gradient in quality leading up to and away from *Only The Lonely*, and I would be inclined to agree. Yet, for a singer at the pinnacle of his creative powers, stealing vertiginous glimpses at private human truths at once arrestingly beautiful and cripplingly bleak, it is also true what they say: it sure is lonely at the top.

Alex Neilson is a UK musician

Stavanger, a coastal town in south west Norway, rarely had
musicians from abroad passing through while I was growing
up. In fact, when I was a kid it was a big deal to meet anyone
from abroad at all. Every year a travelling funfair set up in
an ice rink parking lot near my home, and in the evening it
hosted entertainment for the big kids over 16. In 1980, aged
seven, consumed by an itchy curiosity, I went exploring.
Sporting heavy duty bright yellow Helly Hansen raingear
(daily uniform in Norway), I sneaked out in the pouring
spring rain ready to discover what adults did at night. I
remember hearing loud music, high voices and cars revving.
It all sounded so threatening. To get in was easy: I climbed
under the makeshift stage from the back, and sat there for a
while watching the thundering bass making the scaffolding
tremble. I sat shaking, afraid to be discovered but defiant and
triumphant after breaking into this new terrain. My parents
rarely listened to music involving a drumkit, but here, under
new skies, under a different moon, this sonic holocaust
hovering above me made my blood sing and my skin bump.
What the hell was going on up there?

I slid out the other side unnoticed and took my place in
front of the stage. I thought I'd seen the future: four people
dressed in silvery white illuminated by red and green lights
and with this smoke everywhere. Bodies fading in and out of
the coloured haze, writhing and wriggling in ways I'd only seen
glimpses of on the single TV channel Norway had at the time.

The four musicians were black. I'd never seen a black
person in real life before. I don't think there were any in
Stavanger at that time. They looked so fantastically cool, their
big hair a complete mystery — how did it stay up like that by
itself? Later I was told they were called Boney M. What did
'Boney M' mean? I'm still not sure, but what it meant to me
at the time was a taste of something exotic, and a notion that
music could convey all kinds of meanings and conceal various
mysteries.

Six years later I had cast off my Helly Hansen and was sporting a different me: one entirely dictated by Run DMC. I was so proud of my shiny white Adidas shorts, three blue stripes on either side, and a Run DMC 'My Adidas' T-shirt. Because I had a cool brother who owned all their records and — crucially — a record player, I knew pretty much all the lyrics. I could diss the boys in school any time, by reciting Run DMC lyrics: *'My Adidas and me, close as can be/We make a mean team, my Adidas and me/We get around together, down forever/And we won't be mad when we're caught in bad weather'*.

The title track of 1988's *Tougher Than Leather* spelled out their fabric of choice: rock 'n' roll jackets topped off the rap streetwear. Indeed, they were dubbed by some 'The Beatles of hiphop' (hilariously denied on 1985's 'King Of Rock': *'Every jam we play, we break two needles/There's three of us but we're not The Beatles'*). The trio resided in the New York borough of Hollis, Queens, and were fighting a whole raft of wars: race, gun crime, gangs, drugs, as well as chipping away at the barrier between rock and rap. The unforgettable video for 'Walk This Way' is a perfect visualisation of their barrier-breaking qualities. Aerosmith and Run DMC are each rehearsing, divided by a thin wall, competing over volume. Suddenly, Aerosmith's singer Steven Tyler smashes through the wall followed by Joe Perry in mid-guitar solo, combining a tongue-wiggling, screaming lick with Jam Master Jay's beats. 'King Of Rock' had foretold that video and the trio's ambition: *'Now we crash through walls, cut through floors/Bust through ceilings and knock down doors'*.

Very much the loner in early teenagedom, I felt I was one of those people who were never invited anywhere. When Run DMC blasted a hole in that wall, they also pierced a hole in my perception of myself back then. They helped me build an iron defence against the name-calling and subtle bullying that inevitably accompanies teenage life. Magically, they made me believe in myself. Be proud, you're special, they said, in no uncertain terms. Their initial target audience might have been the residents of Queens, but that didn't mean their words didn't resonate over the Atlantic, ringing in the ear and lighting a fuse inside a little white girl in a little white town feeling excluded from all the fun that other kids seemed to be having. 'Proud To Be Black' on the 1986 masterpiece *Raising Hell* spells it out: *'I ain't no slave, I ain't baling no hay/We're in a tight position in any condition/Don't get in my way, 'cause I'm full of ambition/I'm proud to be black, and I ain't taking no crap/I'm fresh out the pack, and I'm proud to be black'*, and then their trademark, signing off the rhymes in declamatory unison: *'SO TAKE THAT!'*.

It had never occurred to me that I didn't have to put up with being called names. That's how things were; that felt like the role I was expected to play. Run DMC told me I could bark back, that I didn't have to hide. Such a simple message, but back in 1986 at 14, it was an earth shattering, paradigm shifting revelation. It's basic stuff, but kids can reveal an evil streak, and from that moment on Joe Simmons (Run), Darryl McDaniels (DMC) and DJ Jason Mizell (Jam Master Jay) became my three wise American uncles telling me to stand up for myself: have the courage of your convictions, make your own story, believe in yourself rather than authorities and packs of kids. Having the confidence to know who you are. It led to my first kiss, from another hiphop obsessive at school (we called him 'Bag'). I remember wondering whether he actually liked me, or maybe he was kissing me because he knew my brother owned all the Run DMC albums. Who knows? All together now: *'Because it's like THAT, and that's the way it is, HUH!'* .

Anne Hilde Neset is Artistic Director of Norway's nyMusikk organisation

GENESIS BREYER P-ORRIDGE ON THE PSYCHEDELIC DESIGNS OF HAPSHASH AND THE COLOURED COAT

In 1967 I was living in Solihull, Warwickshire, attending public school on a scholarship and becoming increasingly alienated from the young, idly rich buckaroos whom I knew would be my future enemies as fully trained 'future leaders' of the British establishment. I had moved from the Manchester/ Liverpool axis of beat music in 1964 to a place I later described as the 'most sterile place in England'. I was miserable and angry, but I had a secret weapon — I had discovered the beatniks. Jack Kerouac and William S Burroughs had excited me beyond belief, and encouraged me to search for drugs and wild experiences.

One weekend, wandering through Mell Square, I saw a bright pink magazine cover unlike anything I had ever seen before. It turned out to be issue three of *OZ* magazine, and I used every penny I had to buy it. Inside was a raucous, insanely psychedelic battering of agit prop anger, sexual liberation and underground information that was as vital to my development as an artist as seeing a Max Ernst collage had been years earlier. One of the house artists at *OZ* was Martin Sharp, the Ozstralian graphic genius, the other a mysteriously named collective called Hapshash And The Coloured Coat. I became a street seller of *OZ*. That meant I got my copy free by selling extra copies to my close circle of friends, like Spydee Gasmantel III, who were exploring sex, poetry and hashish with me. In the suburbs in 1967, using what we now call recreational drugs rather than the speed pills of the local mods was still a highly dangerous and extreme pastime. Any additional profits went on scoring more hash in Birmingham or from Ron Skinner and Big Baz, our two local beatniks. God knows why they ended up in Solihull!

It was while I was waiting near Birmingham's Bullring for Spydee to return from his connection that I entered a tiny record shop and began browsing through the 'Underground' section. Finding the new trippy music was depressingly difficult for us, and usually required hitchhiking to the Arts

Lab in London's Drury Lane, or the Brighton Combination. On this day I struck audiovisual gold. The most complex, tasteful yet mindblowing album cover I had ever seen was at the front of a bin. It was sealed, but because of my *OZ* connection, I recognised the cover art. It was by Hapshash And The Coloured Coat and the album was credited to Hapshash And The Coloured Coat Featuring The Human Host And The Heavy Metal Kids.

Surprisingly, as I look at it again today, the smiling Buddha/baby sun in the centre looks scarily like the one in *Teletubbies*. Which kind of makes sense, because on the second Hapshash album, Mike Batt (of *The Wombles* theme tune infamy) was a member and coproducer. On one side, the images and lettering were normal; on the other, a mirror split the same graphics down the centre, sucking the eye into a vortex with an effect of myriad layers of glass. Art deco clouds cut by sunrays hark back to the ugly pseudo-stained glass designs over front doors all over suburbia. Cartoon characters like Little Bo Peep appear, too, along with a sense of mutant Victoriana that suggests the crumbling British Empire turning into a meaningless facade.

This ironic debauchery of British colonial exploitation through military might and deception was mined as a vein of imagery over and over by Hapshash and other UK psychedelic artists, combining a sense of loss of power with a bitter manipulation through appropriation. Yet there is also a simultaneous experience of lovingness, attachment and sentimentality, a feeling that even as the artists are deconstructing their past, they remain fond of its simplicity, aware that things can never be the same after the splitting of the atom in the material world and the splitting of the mind in the perceptual, post-acid world. This may well be why they added The Human Host to the name of this musical project. The Host, or the flesh of Christ, is taken at communion, which creates another level of meaning casting the new drugs as a contemporary sacrament.

Looking at this marvel, my eyes were ravished by fresh colour combinations, an entirely new (to me) method of collage creating collisions, overlays and contradictions that immerse and overwhelm reason to simulate delirium. The Burroughs/Gysin cut-up method does a similar thing with writing, which Burroughs always asserted was '50 years behind painting'. The phrase 'Heavy Metal Kid' comes from Burroughs's early 60s *Nova Trilogy*, so there is no doubt in my mind that these guys were acknowledging the cut-up's influence. Information, music and a supreme retinal immersion all combine in this cover, suspending my disbelief and giving space to my sense of infinite possibility and infinite impossibility. I was liberated, and committed to an unorthodox, alternative questioning lifestyle for the rest of my time on Earth, as I spent my ill-gotten gains from *OZ* and became a disciple of the exploration of consciousness, perception and experience.

As for the music, the legend goes that it came about when a rich hippy donated money for an 'acid test' party in a recording studio, with Hapshash assigned to arrange everything. Word had already leaked over to Britain about Ken Kesey's experiments with total improvisation of mind, music and light. Performing on this album are the core of Hapshash, Nigel Weymouth and Michael English (who went on to design the 'big lips' logo for The Rolling Stones); DJ and manager Guy Stevens later played in Art, whose album Jimi Hendrix produced and who later changed their name to Spooky Tooth; Mickey Finn of T-Rex fame jammed, and even Tony McPhee of The Groundhogs was an occasional member. There was at least one solo album later by The Heavy Metal Kids, who were in turn closely linked to The Deviants.

You can still buy the album on CD. However, the smaller cover doesn't really do the artwork justice. Luckily, I still have my original, in gorgeous red vinyl, with a silver and black poster of the group. It was the first time I had ever seen coloured vinyl. The music is very much of its time, which is why all aficionados of psychedelic music history should have a copy. This is a pure, unadulterated gem displaying the initial fervour, optimism and faith in change over submission to fear that fuelled the best part of the underground community.

Genesis Breyer P-Orridge is a UK born musician and artist

Is there any more voluptuous, terrible moment in rock guitar
than the shivery micro-dot pause between initial wah-wah
greeting and immanent storm of sound that baptises then
launches this long-ago and yet-to-come 'Voodoo Chile'?
Hendrix's curlicued intro sounds like a transcription of
electricity itself, a spectral bouncing ball leading us into some
nerveless hieroglyphic beyond... like a long ragged ceremony
has reached its peak and the Other — in some hitherto
unknown, reliably feral shape — will finally deign to speak in
this other tongue.

Epiphany as eclipse. A hiss of radiation and a sturm/
strum of electric gnosis and then this whole new kind of
matrix spun out from six strings and a voice. Sound of
something jettisoned. Sound of gravity turned in on itself.
Sound of air rush, cosmic fire searching for a place to land,
earth itself. Sound when lightning strikes stagnant pool
and DNA wriggles alive, catches its own tail, sparks, goes
from inert parasite to first appearance. Sound of technology
stretched into a new 4D plan of space-time. Sound of the
body's material being wrenched out of one state into another:
a freefall, diabolic other side.

'Voodoo Chile' — it is now staggering to recall — went
straight to Number One, top of the early 70s pops! As a
Track 45 it had been rushed out to commemorate/cash in on
Hendrix's recent death. It was an old track (and an unlikely
single), but it sounded like a whole new world of pleasure
and/or pain to me: like a voice from some Elsewhere I never
suspected existed, somewhere right out on the perimeter of
what pop or rock — or indeed, life — might be. Back then I
didn't much like The Beatles or Beatles-style groups; after
this hoodoo masque of intermittent good/bad vibrations,
they sounded like paint-by-numbers figurines, museum
pieces, Gilbert and Sullivan to Hendrix's Wagner or Mahler.
In Hendrix's hands, rock went beyond polite harmony & solo
into meltdown, overheat, supernova. If most riff and rock

was vaguely militaristic, this was a carnal billowing, a tantric breath. A palindromic oo-D-oo.

For all that's been been said — pro and contra — about Hendrix as supposed phallocrat, this seems to miss (or overstress) the point. If the guitar was an extension of anything, it was surely his tongue. (With the whammy bar as substitute wand.) Oral magician, he spoke the neglected shadow side of blues, the side where the guitar tricks up a foggy re-presentation of Nature: midnight drizzle, back-roads howl, trudge, electric wind. And on 'Voodoo Chile' he conjures a storm there's no escaping from. A cry both bleak and carnal, a Mobius striptease, an intergalactic Blues, this is rock song as lift-off excuse for sonic OD, inexcusable excess, hubristic flight.

'Voodoo Chile' revealed to me (not that I consciously knew it at the time) that sound could speak for itself, that sonic texture/tone could speak as vividly as any lyric, that the sometime novelty of rock/pop could be deliriously serious, could touch (and jar) your very being. In Hendrix's hands, the gadgetry of rocky showmanship was rewired into serious neoterics; into the hint of a new sign system, into assignations with fate, race, destiny, pain; lines of flight and lift off. On 'Voodoo Chile', Hendrix sounds like Benjamin's angel of history blown into the future backwards by a storm of sound.

But really, Hendrix was less a soundtrackist to tribal politics (you know: the same old TV documentary footage of race riots or Vietnam overlaid with Hendrix or Stones) than the first black man in space. In real time, he'd dribbled into death surrounded by debris and detritus (human, chemical, musical, legal). His group was crap. His friends were dubious. His intake was slack rather than sulphurous — more Brian Jones than Papa Legba. He was going grey before he died. (Unlike Miles, say, it didn't seem entirely likely that he had many new trajectories to explore: he appeared to have given way too much already.) But symbolically, sonically, he was in another orbit entirely: for one last split second on 'Voodoo Chile', a gust of cosmic debris awhirl around his head, he pointed a way for others to follow.

I was a little white boy in unsulphurous un-black Norfolk
when this eagle settled on my head and pecked at my ears;
when this coyote howl blooded my curiosity. (Even his name
seemed to ring otherwise — that first name with its trailing
graffiti tail of 'i', where the more rounded proprietorial 'my'
usually plumply sat; and a proper name that ended, all too
inevitably now, it seemed, in 'x'.)

And so the child, an innocent with ears of emptiness,
is hit by an aural lightning flash, initiated into the Electrick
Mysteries by the wand of a magician with antennae hair
and a left hand way. *'I'm a voodoo chile'*, sings this shadow,
this thief, this king, eliding the child you still are into a
phantasmal adult you might just become. Maybe the child
will spend the rest of its life trying to revive or retrieve the
blissful shudder of a revelation.

A child can only be seduced if he or she is shown hints
of knowledge just beyond their comprehension — and then
may spend a lifetime working out the consequences of this
premature entry. Too much to be held back, the epiphany
breaks the picture of what you thought you knew... and when
it recedes, it takes you with it. You are mine now, said this
Voodoo trip/trope: here is your future in a grain of sound.
An on/off chill that hooked me into a whole spread of
intentions beyond my immediate ken. A future marked out in
feedback. Sheer mirage, purple haze, black heart. Epiphany
as eclipse.

Epiphany — it's no laughing matter. This thing that took
my breath away, and marked me through the ear, for life,
was it too much, too soon? I don't know. I do know that ever
since 'Voodoo Chile' the wah-wah has always had a direct
line straight to my psyche. And that ever since 'Voodoo
Chile' there was... a taste for the forbidden and an ache for
codes; a need to go beyond, to look behind. And sometimes
I think I've only ever been working out the consequence
— the non-sequential logic, the dare, the lure, the lunge,
the abyssal spell — of that moment ever since. Sometimes I
think everything that has surprised or seduced me since —
semiotics, magick, voodoo, sonics as erotics, all my angels
and daemons, excuses and blessings, all the dub echo and

deconstructive tremble — was here in a little DNA spiral, the wah-wah code of this voodoo phial. *'Lord knows...'*.

Ian Penman is a UK music critic

CHRIS PETIT ON THE FLEETING PLEASURES OF THE
SINGLE EVOCATIVE SONGLINE

With songs it was always the words, a phrase or line delivery
(*'She said softly, it's best not to linger'*), and in a world that
can never be too laconic, good writers didn't mess around:
there were so many people you just had to meet without your
clothes. Stuck writing books or banished for weeks to film
cutting rooms, you dream of being able to write something
that starts *'Since my baby left me'* or *'It was fun for a while'* and
it's over before you hit the bottom of the page.

I always preferred songs on the radio. By the 1970s we all
had record players, and albums became the main currency,
but they were never great value because there were usually
only a couple of good tracks. Everyone was seduced by *Sgt
Pepper's* but I remember thinking: there's nothing here I'll
be listening to in five years. Maybe because it was what I
grew up with — I liked singles and charts, and the fact that
before Radio 1 and pirate radio, the music was hard to
find. I wondered furiously what a song with the title 'Long
Distance Information' might be about. I first heard it on Radio
Luxembourg, which broadcast only at night and you listened
in the dark, under bedcovers, with an earplug and variable
reception that reduced whole sections of songs to static. Later
on, music turned driving into a movie. Whoever had the idea
of putting a radio in a car was a genius, and whoever thought
of adding a cassette was even more of one. Compared to the
jukebox, the radio was considered an inferior artefact, so I
was grateful to Van Morrison for the line, *'Elvis did not come
in without those wireless knobs'*. I first heard that song ('In The
Days Before Rock 'N' Roll', a title up there with Chuck Berry's)
on a car radio, driving alone at night, thinking, what is this?
And I'm searching for Luxembourg, Athlone, Budapest, AFN,
Hilversum, Helvetia.

I was never interested in live performance (dreary
soundchecks; too much preening; compulsory lateness; and
jerks who clapped and whistled as soon as they recognised
a tune), only the disembodied voice. The randomness of

radio selection, albeit to a formula, put you in the moment. I developed a tolerance for British pop, the stuff you're not supposed to like: 'Here Comes My Baby (With Another Man)'; Dusty Springfield; 'Bend Me, Shake Me'; 'When You Walk In The Room'. Others discussed the merits of Hendrix's and Dylan's versions of 'All Along The Watchtower', a song which never engaged me until its last line — *'Two riders were approaching, the wind began to howl'*. Now with Dylan I always end up returning to his discredited middle period ('Series Of Dreams'; 'Brownsville Girl'; 'Gotta Serve Somebody'), and lines like *'Wasn't thinking of anything specific, nothing too very scientific'* and *'If there's an original thought out there I could use it right now'*.

Part of me always preferred songs as factory product, Cliff Richard to Paul Simon; 'Wired For Sound' rather than 'The Boy In The Bubble'. Songs I went for were usually about people being missing and missed (*'I woke last night and spoke to you, not thinking you were gone and it felt so strange to lie awake alone'*), or they verged on the inarticulate (*'I had a feeling I can't explain'*), with a tension between the certainty of the music and doubts expressed. Morrison's great period of inarticulateness was on *Astral Weeks*: *'The light is on the left side of your hair, and I'm standing in your doorway and I'm mumbling and I can't remember the last thing that ran through my head'*, a line which finds its twin in another highrise setting, Leonard Cohen's 'Tower Of Song': *'I'm standing by the window where the light is strong'*; which also has the magisterial *'I asked Hank Williams how lonely does it get'*.

I listen to very little in its entirety now, other than keeping an ear cocked for the odd line. It's as though the songs have shrunk, whether to do with the songs themselves or age or distance or impatience. Perhaps all that really ever counted was a piece of phrasing that nailed the song in the first place (*'Once upon a time I was falling in love now I'm only falling apart'*), such as the ten or 15 second sequence in Robert Plant's '29 Palms' (again first heard on a car radio), which is gorgeous and quite unlike the rest of a mediocre song. (Ditto Tom Petty's 'Free Falling'.) '29 Palms' mentions radio (*'It becomes quite hard when I hear your voice on the radio'*) and it's about a place I've been. Other radio checks: '*I can see you, your brown skin shining in the sun, you've got the top pulled down, radio on*' (Don Henley); plus The Doors' portentous 'The Wasp (Texas Radio And The Big Beat)', forgiven for its title parentheses, for which I was always a sucker, eg 'It's My Party (And I'll Cry If I Want To)'; 'Nothing's Shaking (But The Leaves On The Trees)'. Place names always disposed me towards a song. Tulsa: '*Something happened to me while I was driving home and I'm not the same anymore*'; Phoenix: '*She'll laugh when she reads the part that says I'm leaving*'; Wichita: '*I hear you singing in the wires and I need you more than want you and I want you for all time*'; Mississippi Bridge ('*About a half a mile from*') and the New Jersey Turnpike ('*In the wee wee hours, driving slowly because of drizzlin' showers*'). Early Van Morrison sang about Notting Hill Gate and the Tottenham Court Road, and The Stones, in anticipation of Mick Jagger's social climbing, mentioned St John's Wood ('*Mother is an heiress*') in 'Play With Fire'.

I struggled through the 1970s. I missed out on The Velvet Underground because I didn't like Lou Reed's voice. A lot came down to that. There was no method to it, just a snap response. I liked the nasal whine of Ray Davies more than Jagger's Thames Delta posturing; preferred Andy Fairweather-Low to Steve Winwood. I would listen to anything by Abba for those two soaring female voices, even the terrible 'Fernando'.

For me, things woke up in the late 1970s with Kraftwerk (music as cinema); with Jonathan Richman's line '*I'm in love with the modern world*'; and Wreckless Eric's 'Whole Wide World' ('*just to find her*'), all of which figured or were referred to in *Radio On*, a film I made in 1979. We also got Bowie singing 'Heroes' ('*And me, I'll drink all the time*') in German, Devo's hopped up version of 'Satisfaction', a dreamy bit of Robert Fripp, and Ian Dury's tribute to Gene Vincent.

In the end, I liked songs that ambushed you. They could come from anywhere, I wasn't fussy: from country ('*Did you ever see Dallas from a DC9 at night?*' and '*Ten years later in Southern California, he met her at a party for a painter; she was naked and sitting in this chair that came from France*'); or Tom

Waits (*'I'm tired of all these soldiers here, no one speaks English and everything is broken... and I'm down on my knees tonight'*); or Blondie (*'Soon turned out to be a pain in the ass'*); or Ray Davies (*'It's your life and you can do what you want, do what you like'*); or Billy Fury (*'I want to be your lover but your friend is all I stay'*).

As for epiphany, I still like references to light, to telephones (*'The operator says 40 cents more for the next three minutes'*); place names (*'One got his Mauser and the other one said, Bangkok'*); radios and photographs (*'It's just a photograph of someone I knew'*); mention of movies and stars (*'I'm standing in line in the rain to see a movie starring Gregory Peck'*); and a sense of trespass and things falling apart (*'Get me out of here, I hate it here'*) and carrying on, and, above all, mobility (*'I'm moving on and from now on address unknown'*).

Chris Petit is a UK film maker and author

Some time in the 1980s I was sitting in an airport lounge in
Minneapolis alongside photographer Peter Anderson. We
had just completed an assignment for a British rock weekly
and were waiting for our connecting flight to London,
when suddenly the airport's PA opened up. 'Will Mr Todd
Rundgren, MR TODD RUNDGREN, please make his way
to the information desk!' Ignoring the last call for our own
flight, I managed to convince Peter that there might be a
good picture up for grabs. Alas the portly, sweating figure
that eventually arrived at the desk bore no resemblance
whatsoever to the Glam God I was hoping to encounter.
Perhaps, on reflection, I had only imagined that I heard his
name being called. We had, after all, once been soul brothers.

Like most impulse buys during my early days of record
collecting in the early 1970s it was the cover that grabbed my
attention first. Todd Rundgren's fourth album, *A Wizard, A
True Star*, came packaged in an elaborate die-cut gatefold
sleeve which looked as though it had been designed by
Salvador Dalí under the influence of some brain melting
hallucinogenic. The cover opened up, magically, to reveal
a picture of Todd scraping shaving foam off his chin from
inside a multi-mirrored dressing room. The reflected clutter
of his surroundings were a subtle pointer to the recorded
chaos that lay within.

A Wizard, A True Star was Rundgren's attempt to
reproduce a psychedelic trip in its entirety on record, an
overly ambitious concept that caused some critics and fans
to wonder what on earth he was playing at. Could this be the
same man who, only one year earlier, had singlehandedly
composed, performed and produced *Something/Anything?*,
a sublime double album of truly original pop music that saw
Rundgren being hailed as the new Brian Wilson? Surely not!
A Wizard, A True Star confounded others with its playing
time. It was too short to run to another double, yet slightly too
long for a single album release. This meant that the volume

had to be constantly cranked up in order to experience the compacted grooves of Todd's audio trip at a reasonable level. Despite this undeniable flaw, my fledgling collector self considered *A Wizard, A True Star* to be a major work and dutifully filed it in my collection alongside other 1973 classics such as The Stooges' *Raw Power*, Blue Öyster Cult's *Tyranny And Mutation* and the Rundgren produced debut from The New York Dolls.

What appealed to me about Todd's *Wizard* was its diversity and the fact that he wasn't afraid to openly experiment, even if the results occasionally blew up in his face. But the section that really impressed me was the medley of soul songs that constituted the highlight of side two.

Pre-Todd, sweet soul music did nothing for me. My Party Seven-fuelled friends would reel ecstatically around some stranger's living room every time 'Reach Out (I'll Be There)' or 'Sex Machine' hit the Dansette. But although I could hear the passion and thrust of these songs, to my ears they sounded so corny and predictable that I found it difficult to fully submit to what they had to offer. But just as it took Frank Zappa and The Mothers Of Invention to fully introduce me to the delights of doo-wop though their *Cruising With Ruben & The Jets* album, so Todd's passionately performed versions of Curtis Mayfield's 'I'm So Proud', Smokey Robinson's 'Ooh Baby Baby' and his own heart tugging 'Sometimes I Don't Know What To Feel' opened my eyes and ears to soul power. Soon after I found myself lingering around the soul rack of my local record dive, desperately searching for the promised musical treasures secretly stacked behind Todd's soul medley. After several weeks of listening intently to the works of Al Green, Curtis Mayfield, Otis Redding and Wilson Pickett, together with a cheapo compilation called *This Is Soul*, I failed miserably to find anything that sent me into a similar state of transcendental bliss.

I was by now a hardened vinyl junkie and soul was proving too soft a drug for my thrill-hungry imagination to absorb. I traded what I had already bought for a batch of Blue Cheers, admitted defeat and returned to 'Search And Destroy'. Todd's pure encapsulation of the music on *A*

Wizard, A True Star, however, continued to haunt me. As did much of Rundgren's previous and later work, which I began to feverishly track down long after my brief flirtation with soul music had ended. A friend sold me her copy of Nazz's first album (Todd's early Beatles-styled garage band), and copies of *The Ballad Of Todd Rundgren* (where he appears on the cover sitting at a piano with a noose around his neck), *Runt* and the aforementioned *Something/Anything?* were quickly added to my growing vinyl pile. Hungry for even more Todd product, I was delighted when I walked into my regular record haunt one day, to be handed an import copy of his latest, a double album called *Todd*. I ran home with it and played it to death.

   Todd was virtually the last of his records I took seriously. I went on to study graphic design at London's Royal College of Art, while he formed Utopia, a monstrous, stadium swelling group whose pretentious jazz rock fusion roar swamped out the forlorn and soulful Rundgren sound I had instantly adored. After he delivered one last great solo album called *Hermit Of Mink Hollow* in 1978, my spiritual relationship with his music ground to a halt, and I started listening to Albert Ayler instead.

Edwin Pouncey is a UK music journalist. His alter ego is the cartoonist and graphic artist Savage Pencil

Time in the countryside almost functions not at all, and
if and when it does, it usually serves to remind you that,
unfortunately, you're still there. The empty time of rural life
— empty, that is, if you're not working on the land or serving
feudal lords by trapping grouse for them — is inherently
estranging, even if you are remotely inclined to revel in this
desolate timelessness. Aware that there is a world elsewhere,
clocks seem to stop, history ends, and *The Archers* seems to be
on all the fucking time.

There's a way in which 'teen angst', perhaps best
understood as a combination of a perfectly rational distaste
for the status quo combined with a deep uncertainty about
one's own relation to whatever might conceivably be
understood to belong to you — your body, your thoughts —
gets played out in confusing ways, regardless of whether you
live in a village, suburbia or cities that people have actually
heard of. The 1990s — just like the 2010s — felt politically and
culturally regressive in many ways, from Oasis's blokeish,
selfish bullshit ('*Where were you when we were getting high?*')
to the attacks on modes of protest and social critique
(feminism, anti-racism, talk of class? Are you mad?).

Immersed in this deep, static form of rural eternity, I
was sadly too young for rave, but it was clear that at least
something was happening in Wiltshire, with people coming
from everywhere to be at Avebury, Stonehenge, West Kennet
Long Barrow, or just a field somewhere. And the poll tax had
been defeated! Underneath the Tory boredom of everyday
life and the cultural dominance of atrocious Beatles copyists,
there was hope for the revolutionary past of the British
countryside — and for music, too.

I faintly recall reading a review of Fugazi's *Red Medicine*
in one of the music papers at the time it came out in 1995,
which described the opening few bars of the record as the
sound of suitcases being chucked down a flight of stairs.
Compared to what was being played on Radio 1's *The Evening*

Session, which I listened to obsessively in the mid-90s, even though it was awful, this sounded promising: and indeed, it was. By no means Fugazi's most critically acclaimed album — it has been unjustly neglected since its release — *Red Medicine* was a revelation: a potentially impossible mix of abrasion and dub mingled with lyrics that felt simultaneously cold and sexy (*'Your eyes like crashing jets/Fixed in stained glass/But not religious/You should pay rent in my mind/Say like the French say bonsoir regret a demain'*). The jolts and false starts of the opening track never fail to terrify and excite.

Compared to the dreariness of Britpop, Fugazi were extraordinary: how could anger sound this attractive? The isolation and boredom of the countryside was somehow broken by the sound of Brendan Canty, Joe Lally, Ian MacKaye and Guy Picciotto telling the truth: *'The answer is there, the answer is there but there is not a fixed position'*. It was my first proper lesson in dialectics! Red medicine indeed... The tendency teenagers have to turn inwards, to try to fix the world while feeling deeply uncomfortable in their own being, seemed drawn into stark relief whenever this record was on. Oscillating between negative affects, guilt, self-renunciation, self-imposed punitive self-education (Maoism in one person!), and a desire to do precisely what Minor Threat told us we couldn't do, Fugazi encapsulated to my teenage self the very contradictions that made life so seemingly difficult. And they even understood insomnia: *'You will sleep forever/You will never sleep again'* ('Fell, Destroyed'). I loved them, but not in a romantic way, of course!

Wide awake much too often, having never been able to work out how to sleep properly, Fugazi made it very clear that the problem — problems, rather — was far less about a personal failing to get on with things and stop being cross all the time, than a set of structural wrongs: the cops, prisons, Lockheed Martin Marietta and the end of a certain political sequence (*'I'm channelling 17 dead revolutions'*). But their politics weren't obvious, or at least, if they eventually were, they needed unpicking, subtly, like a cryptic crossword clue. What little I knew or could find out about them in the pre-internet world, about the politics of the group, their history and the distribution system of Dischord, appealed too: cut out the middleman, stay alert, remain true. The allusive way in which *Red Medicine* picks out and humorously plays with a certain political desire and contradictory aesthetic framework (*'It's cold outside and my hands are dry skin cracked and I realise that I hate the sound of guitars'*) clarified things precisely by making them more complicated. *Red Medicine* breaks language across its strange instruments, mingles love songs with political outrage and fills the whole thing with a sense of soft, sweet languor, despite, or perhaps because of, its wiry intensity. *Red Medicine* was, and still is, both the diagnosis and the cure.

Nina Power is a UK Senior Lecturer in Philosophy at Roehampton University

How do pop groups choose their fans? Like any romance, it's
a subtle, near-imperceptible process of sifting through the
general population, a trail of lures and signals. I'm still not
sure what it was that seduced me into a long infatuation with
Scritti Politti: the sound or the idea of the group. Back in 1979,
the two were inseparable, of course. The urgencies of the post-
punk era made the notion of music-for-music's-sake seem
decadent, trivial, absurd. And some of the best groups were
more influential as concepts than fully realised propositions.

What grabbed my ear first was the name, I think. Just
the sound of it: Scritti Politti, brittle and chiming like the
guitar sound on 'Bibbly O Tek' (first Scritsong I ever heard,
on John Peel, late 1979). That, and the sheer intrigue of
what it might refer to. Eventually I discovered that it was a
slight corruption of the title of a book by neo-Marxist thinker
Antonio Gramsci. Which only enhanced the image I'd already
gleaned from the music press of this shadowy collective
operating at some fabulously uncompromising and far
reaching outer limit of politics and pop. If even Paul Morley,
reviewing two of their singles for *NME*, found them faintly
forbidding, well, count me in!

If I'm really honest, though, I think it was a photo that
sealed the deal: vocalist Green Gartside dragging on a cigarette, thin as a rail inside his baggy jumper. Clearly teetering
on the edge of his nerves, with what looked like kohl darkly
etched around his fragile, blazing eyes, he seemed the incarnation of intensity — all the glamour of a life harrowed by
thought. There was another figure in the photograph (or was
it another picture altogether?), a white guy with blonde dread-
locks: back then, this was quite a striking fashion statement
(nowadays, it just signifies 'nu metal, yuk!'). The 4 *A-Sides*
EP was the first Scritti release I actually got hold of: a 12"
single (exotic in 1979 — at least if you lived in a Hertfordshire
commuter town), with typography that mimicked a reggae
pre-release (except Scritti wrote 'Pre-Langue', a pre-echo of

Green's soon come Derridean preoccupation with language). On the front, another intriguing photo: Scritti's communal squat in Mornington Crescent, North London. A framed hammer and sickle above the mantelpiece harked back to Green's past as a Young Communist, although somebody has sacrilegiously hung what looks like a teabag or tampon off the sickle. The place is a tip: empty beer bottles, typewriter with a tower of books piled on top, 7" single nailed to a wall densely covered with flyers, broadsheets, activist pamphlets. On the back cover, a breakdown of the EP's recording costs, plus phone numbers for label printers, pressing plants, etc: demystification of the means of production, designed to encourage/enable others to do it themselves.

Green later loudly disowned the music of *4 A-Sides* and the two other 'earIy Scritti' releases, but I still find it thrilling. 'Skank Bloc Bologna', the debut single, is a desolate, desperate ballad for exiles on the High Streets of Babylon UK, its loping punky-reggae riddim overlaid with a clangour of close-chorded guitar and pierced by plangent carillon lead runs that some sages claim are steeped in the influence of Martin Carthy-era Steeleye Span. I found the song title wonderfully mysterious and evocative. Now, knowing more about the period, I wonder if it was some kind of 'answer' to ATV's 'Alternatives To NATO': an imaginary network of dissidents stretching from Jamaica to Bologna's anarchist squatters, via Ladbroke Grove (on the B side, the frantic instrumental '28/8/78' is overlaid with a TV news report on that year's rioting at Notting Hill Carnival).

4 A-Sides is first phase Scritti at their peak. There is palpable joy and fervour in the playing. Pace Gramsci, the rhythm section — Tom Morley (the guy with natty dreads) and Niall Jinks — provide 'the optimism of the will' to counter the lyrics' 'pessimism of the intellect'. Jinks's bass, squirming and writhing, is simultaneously the music's funk motor and melodic focus. And Green's minor key twists and multitracked vocal babble can't hide his gifts as singer and tunesmith. The words, oscillating line by line between theoretical abstraction and the concrete quotidian details of everyday oppression, are as far beyond Gang Of

Four's schematic case studies of false consciousness as that group was an advance on Tom Robinson's 'tell it like it is' protest. 'PA's', for instance, moves back and forth between Scritti's struggle to exist (rehearsal costs, debts, bailiffs) and fascism in 1920 and 1933: the mystery of popular support for totalitarianism, all its daft pageantry and atavistic ritual. *'How did they all decide?'*, wonders Green. *'What was irrational/Is national!'*, he states, before imagining, with tres 1979 paranoia, the same thing happening in the UK, land of moderation.

I've never written a letter to a pop musician, but I nearly wrote one to Green in the summer of 1980. I was going to tell him that he was a melodic genius and should just go for it, full-on POP. I could hear something in songs like 'Confidence' (all Motown handclaps and plaintive blue-eyed soulfulness) that screamed Top Ten, but I couldn't put my finger on it. Maybe I'd just assimilated some of the early music press chatter about entryism, ambition, aiming for the charts. But I still feel a shiver of clairvoyance when I recall playing *C81* (a cassette compilation of independent music put together by *NME* and Rough Trade) for the first time, spring 1981. For there, on track one, was Green unveiling his New Pop direction with the luscious lovers rock of 'The 'Sweetest Girl'', the nectar of his voice finally freed from the thorny tangles of early Scritti's self-deconstructing sound.

'Faithless', glorious PoMo soul, followed swiftly, along with interviews galore in which Green couched his shift to pop in terms of health, an escape from morbid and moribund marginalism. When a third single failed to chart, though, Green abandoned Rough Trade shortly after 1982's debut album *Songs To Remember*, and signed to Virgin. Along with the independent ideal, he junked Scritti's last vestiges of collectivism, firing his group, and restructuring it as a solo vehicle in all but name. And he reinvented his sound for a third time: totally modern electro funk, all chattering sequencers and hypergloss keyboards. 'Wood Beez' and 'Absolute' were stunning hit singles, still haunted by the old Scritti's melodic eeriness. Finally a proper popstar, Green disappeared into the studio and racked up huge bills recording the sequel to 1985's *Cupid & Psyche 85*. I interviewed him circa 1988's *Provision* (the first time his ideas/sound hadn't moved on significantly), and found him rather smug. (Best to avoid meeting your heroes, on the whole.) Again, he disappeared for an eternity, bunkered down in a cottage in his native Wales, only to return in 2000 with an unfortunate Grunge-meets-Amish goatee and confused rap-influenced comeback *Anomie & Bonhomie*. I still wonder sometimes whatever happened to bassist Niall and Tom the dreadlocked drummer.

Simon Reynolds is a UK born music critic and author

There were a lot of strikes in the 1980s: the Miners' Strike, the Printers' Strike; even my schoolteachers went on strike in protest at the Conservative government's attempts to make education serve the needs of industry rather than students. And, many rungs down the ladder of national importance, I went on strike too, against pop music. With more than the average pomposity of adolescence, I decided that there were too many records, too many DJs asking me to get excited about Johnny Hates Jazz or even The Jesus And Mary Chain.

What good was music in the face of the coming apocalypse? I threw away my back issues of *NME*, vowed never to watch *The Tube* again and moved the radio dial to Radio 4 where, for reasons long forgotten, I felt I could best serve the cause of revolutionary socialism by listening to afternoon plays about elderly divorcees trying to settle into rural life in Chichester. That was until I first laid hands on a copy of a Bristol based fanzine entitled *Are You Scared To Get Happy*.

Are You Scared To Get Happy, its name taken from Hurrah!'s 1983 song 'Hip Hip', was like nothing I had seen before. I was too young to know about 1970s zines such as *Sniffin' Glue*, and in the small town of Gloucester where I grew up there were no clubs or music venues outside which more recent titles might have been sold. The groups being lionised — Remember Fun, Blackcurrant Dexedrine — meant nothing to me, but that didn't matter; I was mesmerised by the ardour and fury of the writer, Matt Haynes, whose prose heaved with gerunds — trembling, surging, cascading — and abounded with capital letters and exclamation marks.

Each page was a riot of colour, text spilling in all directions and accompanied by lyrics, flowers, pictures of Tube stations, so that they looked like action paintings. There were rarely any group photos; instead there were shots of small town landscapes, dulled topographies reimagined in this context as nascent hotbeds of seething aspiration and redemptive creativity. And rather than interviews or discographies, Haynes would write hungry, wild-eyed manifestos about the importance of vision, belief, love. His was a fierce affirmation, a politics of 'yes-ness': he really seemed to think that words, and the enthusiasm they conveyed, would bring into being his ideal pop republic.

The fanzine, like many at that time, came with a free flexidisc featuring Baby Lemonade and The Bachelor Pad, but I wasn't able to play it. Not owning a record player during my adolescence meant that I had to tape favourite songs off the radio using an old 70s cassette recorder; listen carefully to my home recordings of Big Flame's 'Cubist Pop Manifesto' or McCarthy's 'Frans Hals' and you'll hear the ambient leakage of passing ice cream vans or of my mother yelling at me to come downstairs and eat my dinner. And so, even though I've still to this day never heard a note by Baby Lemonade, I knew then, through the intensity of Haynes's prose and its teeming, glorious imagery which made me shake as I read it, that this record was life transforming.

I started skipping school dinners, sending the money I saved to obscure addresses in Penzance, Didsbury and Penge, from where, weeks later, I would receive small packages containing combustible, inflated language about outfits such as Bob, The Siddeleys and Jesse Garon & The Desperadoes. Conventional pop history damns their music, and indeed the scene around them, as twee and reactionary. I adored their trebly romanticism, as well as their repudiation of blokey rock tropes and noise strategies, all of which seemed to me to mirror rather than offer an alternative to the harshness of Anglo-American monetarism.

These groups weren't seceding from society: The Orchids released 'Defy The Law', an anti-Poll Tax song before most people knew what the Poll Tax was, while Haynes railed against 'the monstrous pestles of CAPITALIST GREED', and fanzines such as *Troutfishing In Leytonstone* were full of articles about urban Situationism. Rather, they cultivated an idea of studied innocence, a strategic youthfulness in an era when student grants were being eroded, squat culture was under threat, and the imperative to grow up seemed inseparable from the demand to wear adjustable-collared stripy shirts, buy expensive CDs and not give a damn about American bombs targeting Tripoli.

Are You Scared To Get Happy was catalytic. It was an example of the very thing for which it argued: that it wasn't enough just to consume music, but that you had to make or share it. I was inspired to publish a few fanzines myself, all of them dedicated to joining the dots between anti-racist politics, Latin satirical verse and the more obscure parts of the Cherry Red back catalogue. Lucky the people today who can use pre-existing blog templates to broadcast their passions across the world, but I still harbour fond memories of being forced to break into photocopier rooms or arguing with friends about the ideological implications of printing up essays composed on a typewriter rather than in my own inky scrawl.

The other day, for the first time in 20 years, I looked at a couple of issues of *Are You Scared To Get Happy*, and of other fanzines of the period — *Hungry Beat, Far Out And Fishy, Adventures In Bereznik*. Compared to the '4/5 stars', 'download this', bullet-pointed prose of so much pop discourse these days, they seem almost avant garde. Their editors thought nothing of drawing links between music and art, cinema and politics. They took it for granted that music journalism wasn't just about auteur reverence or thick descriptions of new sounds; it was also about ideas, reading lists, designs for living. It all seems a long time ago, but their passion still assails, their dreams inspire.

Sukhdev Sandhu is a UK born journalist and author

MIKE SHALLCROSS ON BEING SCORCHED BY THE
FIRE OF THE GUN CLUB'S ATAVISTIC AMERICANA

I remember the moment the fire ignited — 1984 or 85 on a
John Peel show. It was as if the song didn't know quite where
to start, grit swirling aimlessly in a dust bowl. *'It's cloudy in
the west, it looks like the rain'*, drawled an American voice,
before an autistic punk groove kicked in. Sounding strangely
archaic, like nothing this suburban Merseyside teenager had
heard before, it was bluesy and wracked with both yearning
and guilt.

While many of the groups on Peel's mid-80s playlist shied
away from the guitar, reducing its roar to apologetic trebly
runs, this record embraced it — not through the fumbling,
masculine virtuosity of the rock solo, but with the siren scale
of the blues slide. Harsh, exotic and sexy, it was a love song
full of insults sung by a bad singer full of soul. Peel identified
it as 'Ghost On The Highway' by The Gun Club. I had a
feeling they were my new favourite group.

At the time they were taking one of their periodic
lay-offs, but that didn't stop the music weeklies sneering
at their overweight drunkard of a lead singer Jeffrey Lee
Pierce. Seeing as the inkies were all in thrall to The Smiths
and The Style Council at the time, however, their disdain
was recommendation enough. For me, Jeffrey Lee was a
true romantic figure, albeit a badly dressed one. Pop culture
fetishises the emaciated child-man, but he was fighting a
half-hearted battle against babyish chubbiness. I took his war
with his appetites as a sign of life. In place of the cavernous
cheekbones of the tortured rock star, Pierce's thick, sensuous
features gave him a strange masculine prettiness. Combined
with the straggling locks he bleached in honour of his
heroine Debbie Harry, you could see why one US magazine
described him as 'Marilyn Monroe from Hell'.

I sought out The Gun Club's three official LPs, *Fire Of
Love*, *Miami* and *The Las Vegas Story*. Far from being the
kind of 'great' albums loved by gong-awarding critics, they
generally sounded like the group had run out of money

midway through the recording — as was often the case. But what they lacked in polish, they compensated for in vision and daring. *Fire Of Love* is bluesy dadaism thrashed out with amphetamine economy, summarised by a brash stop/start reworking of Robert Johnson's 'Preachin' Blues'. Taken at hurricane force, it argues that the blues isn't a state of mind but an ethic. *Miami* is dark country music, scripted by the tangled imagination of Flannery O'Connor. Meanwhile, the lounge metal of *The Las Vegas Story* would be greeted as a bold statement of intent were it released today. Granted, the shambolic Pharoah Sanders and Gershwin covers are ill-conceived, but Pierce's voice always cut through; haphazard in his pitching, he would leap from choral highs to tomb-sombre passages. Quivering and awkward in his phrasing, Jeffrey Lee sang as if words were not his chosen means of expression.

His paradoxes began in the cradle. Born to an all-American father with a great love of the outdoors and a glamour-obsessed Mexican mother, his childhood was scarred by a sense of not belonging to either community, leaving him with feelings of loneliness that dogged his whole life. He developed a wanderlust which, pre-Gun Club, took him to Jamaica to track down reggae musicians. Later he spent many years in London and also developed a fascination with Japan, yet he never really found his natural home. 'I love no country, I am a country!' he once proclaimed.

Musically he was similarly unwilling to pledge allegiances. Pierce raged against the post-punk scene he was lazily linked with. He took the teetotalism of The Sisters Of Mercy's Andrew Eldritch as a personal insult, and he was similarly disgusted when Big Black split up so that guitarist Santiago could go to law school. For Jeffrey Lee music was more a calling than a career option. Doctors advised him to give it up to protect his failing health, but like the protagionist of the American folk song 'John Henry', he pledged to *'keep hitting that hammer till I die'*.

I got to see Gun Club live just once, at Newcastle's Riverside in 1987. Luckily it was the great Gun Club line-up: Pierce's bass-playing girlfriend Romi Mori, guitarist and cofounder Kid Congo (a future Bad Seed), and Clock DVA's drummer Nick Sanderson. With this line-up Pierce cut *Mother Juno*, his masterwork. The production by Cocteau Twin Robin Guthrie mottles the raw Zeppelin guitar riffs and thunderous drum sounds with a cut glass ambience. Guthrie's influence is most heavily felt on 'Breaking Hands'. Based on a dream Pierce had about Romi, who took the solos on the track despite finding the lyrics unbearably intense, it is a huge howl of pain, with the singer sounding weary and alone, a battered angel, hovering over a backdrop of slide guitar and oddly saccharine chimes.

Like all flames, Jeffrey Lee scorched those close to him. His musicians periodically walked out; then, after a decade of turmoil, he split up with Romi. At 29 he was diagnosed with cirrhosis of the liver. But a brief dry period aside, Pierce continued to drink, even as his behaviour became increasingly unpredictable. He once caused a major police alert when he ran riot in a London bar with a samurai sword. He was deported to America soon after. Romi last saw him alive when he was being led through the barriers at Heathrow Airport. When she heard he was in a coma in Salt Lake City, she took the next flight out. Sadly, it was too late. Pierce died of a brain haemorrhage on 31 March 1996. The fire had gone out.

Critically he was forgotten long before. But maybe that's how he would have wanted it. Like the archaic forms of 50s pop swept away by the rise of rock 'n' roll that inspired him, his work lies dormant waiting for a similar spirit to rediscover it. For his send-off Romi organised a Buddhist ceremony. Perhaps Jeffrey Lee still has one eye on a comeback — karma after the storm.

Mike Shallcross is UK Deputy Editor of *Men's Health* magazine

It was the drumming that finally weaned me off hard rock.
Like many schoolboys in the late 1960s, my musical life
revolved around the posturings of skinny youths with
screaming guitars — the sort of musicians I first heard on John
Peel's *Top Gear*, or read about amid the dayglo splutterings
of the underground press. But I was slowly coming to the
realisation that rock, with its over-reliance on leaden tub
thumping, was a cul-de-sac: I sensed that there were other
musics, other worlds, other possibilities. But where?

I grew up in a remote part of Scotland, and finding
interesting records was hard work. Record shops usually
doubled as electrical goods retailers, and stocked only the
Top Ten and a ragbag of Scottish music that suggested
Caledonian musical taste was still defined by Harry Lauder.
Unusual records — weird stuff — had to be bought by mail
order. Charles Lloyd's *Love-In* was an early discovery.
Recorded live at the Fillmore West, it had Jack DeJohnette
on drums — all bristling propulsion and clean rhythmic lines
— and emphatically signposted my road ahead.

I came across DeJohnette again on *Bitches Brew*, an
album I first heard on AFN, the US armed forces radio
network which broadcast to American troops stationed in
Europe. ('And now, a track from the new Miles Davis album,
the title changed for broadcasting purposes to... *Witches
Brew*'). *Bitches Brew* led me to the previous year's *In A Silent
Way*, where I discovered Tony Williams, who seemed even
sharper on the kit than DeJohnette. Between them and the
seething cauldron of Miles's keyboard driven funk, those
albums opened up vistas of rhythmic possibility and provided
a real alternative to the turgidity of rock.

Gig going was as problematical as record buying. I lived
30 miles from Edinburgh, and catching groups live was largely
dependent on the local bus service. When the skinny guitarists
made their occasional visits to Scotland's capital, I was
invariably forced to leave before the end if I was to catch the

last bus home and avoid spending the night in a bus shelter. Despite this, and other impediments, I managed to see enough guitar mangling groups to confirm my suspicion that rock was not the Valhalla most of my generation thought it was.

In the autumn of 1970, The Tony Williams Lifetime came to town. The Lifetime line-up offered an intoxicating blend of rock swagger and jazz precision, and a glimpse of what the groups of the future might sound like as rock and jazz cross-pollinated.

Their most famous member was Jack Bruce, whose keening vocals and 'contrapuntal basslines' (as the lofty-browed reviewers of the time described them) had made him by far the most interesting member of Cream. Only slightly less famous was John McLaughlin, another *Bitches Brew* alumnus, whose slashing, resonant guitar sonics hung over the group like sheet lightning (his 1969 album *Extrapolation* was another of my significant discoveries). In Larry Young, Lifetime had a further link with Miles, and his organ added some of the keyboard squelch that made *Bitches Brew* so immersive. And finally Williams himself, a drummer who sounded like ten thousand insects tap dancing on a tin roof, and whose expressive rhythmic bite effortlessly transcended the foursquare thud of rock.

The Lifetime gig was to transform more than my musical horizons; in fact, it was to have an unforeseen and cataclysmic effect on my post-adolescent life. The gig was on a Sunday night, the least convenient time to do anything in sabbatarian Scotland; a time when a huge black cloud of torpor settled over the entire country and when the bus network was at its most unaccommodating. But, with a friend (he was the ideal companion; he always carried a John Surman album around with him), I arrived at the venue in the heart of the dour capital, sensing that this was to be some sort of musical rite of passage: a moment of revelation. All we had to do, as I constantly reminded my friend, was to leave early to catch the last bus home.

The group surged and raged like a juggernaut on a skidpan. They eclipsed every other live act I had previously seen. The sheer exoticism of the music wormed its way into my nascent musical consciousness. This was real music. So compelling in fact, that the clock was forgotten, and we became transfixed by the huge life-affirming energy rush of Lifetime. We stayed until the roadies switched off the speaker cabinets and the red lights faded out. We stayed until the last bus had been returned to its depot, the engine turned off and the driver gone home to bed.

My friend had a grown-up sister living nearby. We slept on her floor, planning to catch the first bus in the morning and to be in school by 9am. But we overslept, and instead of getting the first bus of the day, we caught a mid-morning one which we took to just beyond the Edinburgh suburbs — those middle class gulags with faux-Baronial architecture and heather-clad gardens that mark the point where the prim city ends and the raw countryside begins. From here, we would hitch a lift and, with luck, be home by lunchtime.

As we trudged through a cold Scottish morning, two cars approached, travelling towards us in the opposite direction. The vehicles slowed as they drew level and I realised, in a moment of icy dread, that we were looking into the eyes of the entire senior teaching staff of our school: every head of every department; every bloody one of them. As the cars crawled past, the occupants stared sullenly at us. They didn't stop. They didn't look back. They just drove past. In slow motion. Dreamlike.

Later, we discovered that the school's departmental heads were on their way to attend the funeral of a previous headmaster. For me, this unlikely encounter was to prove disastrous. My appearance on a stretch of road outside Edinburgh, at a time when I should have been in school, was a misdemeanour too far. I was already on a sort of academic bail as punishment for running an underground school magazine called *Fugg* (named after the East Village musical insurrectionists The Fugs). When I returned the next day, I was expelled.

As my friends dispersed to universities and colleges around the country, I stayed locked in my bedroom, caught in a downcurrent of parental dismay, mild depravity and pharmaceutical self-recrimination. Eventually, I sold my record collection, and took the long road south to London, never to return. In fact, I caught the overnight bus, taking with me only a few favourite albums. *Emergency!* by The Tony Williams Lifetime was among them.

Adrian Shaughnessy is a UK graphic designer, critic and publisher and Senior Tutor in Visual Communication at London's Royal College of Art

I thought I might turn into a pillar of salt. There they were
before me, laid out in dozens of boxes, some 3000 records,
or 30 linear feet in all, comprising a solid half of my record
collection. Scratch that: until the day before, they had been
half of my record collection. But now they were property
of Amoeba Music, the behemoth record store on San
Francisco's Haight Street. They still bore some trace of
me — the boxes were labelled, for the sorters' convenience,
'Electro — Sherburne'. (How strange, that the age-old system
of provenance, more customarily reserved for fine art and
antiquities, should trickle down all the way to black plastic
discs manufactured, in some cases, only a few years before.)
But within a day or so, they would begin filtering out into
Amoeba's already overstuffed shelves, and from there into
new homes, new collections; to be played, saved, sampled,
discarded, or perhaps even resold on eBay, where they'd fetch
the kind of prices I couldn't be bothered to try for. Whatever
their fate, they were no longer mine.

That my records and I should cross paths one more time,
here in the employees-only area of the cavernous record store,
once a bowling alley, was coincidence.

I was here to interview the shop's electronic music
buyer for a documentary film, a last-chance appointment
before I moved from San Francisco to Spain. Well, not
such a coincidence, then — the records had come here to
accommodate my move. My mother generously donated me
basement space in her new condo in Portland, Oregon, but
even maternal generosity has limits. To paraphrase Oscar
Wilde, to sell half one's record collection may be regarded
as a misfortune; to ask one's mother to look after all of it is
carelessness.

I could have kept them all, of course. Could have
imposed upon my mom, or rented storage space, like all good
Americans do. But really, I was excited to reduce my holdings
in heavy, hard-to-move things. As difficult as the selection

was, as I sorted through a collection I'd spent more than two decades filling out, I was relieved to see them go.

Again and again, people who know me — that is to say, people who have seen my messy apartment, where every inch of wall space was occupied by shelving units, where empty album sleeves climbed toward the ceiling, where to get to my desk, you had to step over rows of records filing out from the walls — ask, 'Why? How did you do it?' ('You're not married,' said one of the Amoeba employees who came to appraise my collection, shaking his head.) It's not something I've figured out an answer to yet, really. Only that I knew it was time. The chaos of my collection had come to feel like a burden. The difficulty of locating what I wanted to hear was absurd; finding doubles (or triples) of records I didn't even know I owned single copies of made me feel like any other retail-addicted slob. Discovering albums I hadn't opened by artists I didn't know existed should have offered a sense of possibility, but too often it felt profligate, a reminder that without this ridiculous habit, I might have raised the down payment on a house, or perhaps launched a label of my own.

After all, what's the trade-off between collecting and creating? In the past year I've returned, after 15 years, to making music of my own. Perhaps to compensate for my last Great Unburdening, when at the wise old age of 18 I signed on for the guitarrorist jihad and sold my Korg Poly 800 and Oberheim Matrix-6, I've spent the last eight months giving myself carpal tunnel syndrome twisting the knobs on newly purchased gearboxes. And somehow, when sleeping, eating and doing paid work tie for a distant fourth place to twiddling until dawn, the prospect of poring through my old records doesn't even make it over the finish line.

'Every passion borders on the chaotic, but the collector's passion borders on the chaos of memories.' That's Walter Benjamin writing on book collecting, in an essay obviously applicable to record collectors. Nick Hornby would love the idea, I'm sure, what with his *High Fidelity* protagonist arranging his record collection chronologically by life event. But I've never cared much for that kind of autobiographical impulse; never once did I feel the urge to organise my records by date acquired, though I've often dreamed of ordering them according to the colour of their spines. Call me an aesthete or a would-be amnesiac; it's all the same.

It's anyone's guess as to whether my father was a worse packrat than I. Perhaps it's a blessing that he was deaf; our family home was merely full of trinkets, photographs and rocks — lots of rocks, which my father cut, or polished, or simply let lie in the pebbly driveway, as though returning them to their origins. I'm the one who introduced rock to the house — death rock, punk rock, indie rock. At one point, when I was 15 or so, my mother pulled me aside and said with a scowl, 'Where does your allowance go? If I didn't know better I'd think you were doing drugs.'

She knew better, of course — all she had to do was look at my room, at the stacks of vinyl LPs and copies of *Maximum Rock 'N' Roll* and the posters of Siouxsie and Sonic Youth on the walls, to figure out where that money went.

Shortly before my dad passed away in January 2005, this famous harbourer of objects pulled my mother close. He had fretted about what child or grandkid would get which gew-gaw, but now he only said quietly, his throat clotted with cancer, 'None of it matters.' He gestured towards an imaginary shelf brimming with crap and repeated his pronouncement, the kind of thing one can only know with certainty in the last days of one's life, when a near century's worth of prevarications and relativisms becomes as clear as an eyedropper full of Oxycontin. 'None of this stuff matters.'

And so it was with relief that I cut my holdings in half and watched it be carted off by three young men who strained and cursed under the load. And while it was with some pangs that I encountered 'my' records one more time, there in Amoeba's sorting section, it wasn't without a sense of promise. Imagine that all of these objects of mine could, conceivably, enter 3000 individual homes. My chaos of memories, scrubbed clean and sent off to seed a forest of moments-to-be.

As I was preparing to leave Amoeba's sorting area, my eyes strayed from my orphaned wax to wander over boxes of backstock, falling upon a familiar image: El General, the Panamanian dancehall don. I'd discovered him while backpacking in Ecuador, in 1991. I didn't want to carry the vinyl home, though, so a Quito music shop offered to tape me the record for the price of a blank cassette, plus one dollar. (Sorry, El — I doubt you made much on that deal.) I'd been looking for this record — home to such proto-reggaeton hits as 'Te Ves Buena' and 'Muévalo' — for 14 years now. 'Yo, Mike,' I said, nudging my employee friend. 'Could you price that for me? I need it.' Dutifully, Mike tagged the record — $2.99, not even a dent in what I'd just been paid for my sacrifice. El General grinned up at me from between my eager fingers, his face as ridiculous as my own fixation. I said my goodbyes, hit the cashier and forked over three dollars and change, with tax — and walked out onto Haight Street, 2999 records lighter than I'd come in.

Philip Sherburne is a US born music critic, DJ and producer

MARK WASTELL ON FINDING HIMSELF OVER
DRESSED AND UNDER PREPARED FOR A NIGHT OF
AVANT GARDE JAZZ

Exiting Holborn underground station in central London, the
early evening buzz of people rushing to and fro gripped me
like a vice. Another concert to attend, excited anticipation,
I'm soaking up a lot of live music. Loving it. Sunday 12
March 1989. I'm heading for the Royalty Theatre, a couple
of minutes walk from the station. Never been there before
(or since), but find it easily enough. I enter the building and
then... Bang! What the hell...? This feels different... strange...
uncomfortable even. Now I'm a little nervous. Have I done the
right thing by coming here? I mean, I don't even know these
performers. Never heard a note from any of them. Why was
I here? I'd read about them, quite weighty characters by all
accounts. Lots of coverage in *The Wire*, that magazine seems
to know what's what. It was an advert in the same publication
that piqued my interest in the concert. But look at these
people, the other audience members. Arty types. You know
the sort. They just have that look about them. An overload of
trench coats and army surplus boots. Bad haircuts. Solitary
figures with their heads buried in books before the start of the
concert. Others, huddled in groups, embroiled in animated
conversation. Men mainly. The menacing air of academia
about them. I'm feeling inferior. I'm 20 years old and full of
prejudice, a shining example of the comprehensive school
system. I've been a greengrocer for the last four years. But
these guys, they look like they know things. A lot more than
me, that's for sure. They scare me. Bollocks, what if someone
starts to talk to me? Asks my opinion of one of the performers.
I decide to avert my gaze, trying not to catch anyone's eye.
Hopefully, it won't be too long before the music starts.

We are invited to take our seats. A fair turn out. These
guys must be good to have such a large following. Someone
walks on stage. No announcement. No dimming of the
house lights. Then he puts a soprano saxophone to his lips. I
had never witnessed a solo saxophone performance before,

but I'd heard a lot of good saxophone players. Even in the first couple of months of 1989, I'd seen George Coleman, Steve Williamson, Tommy Smith, Joe Henderson, Dewey Redman, James Moody, Johnny Griffin. Yeah, I was a bit of a jazzhead at the time. Anyway, this guy starts blowing. Then blows some more, then more still. Blow, blow, blow. His fingers are tracing a frantic spider crawl over the instrument. Blowing, blowing, fingering, fingering. And it doesn't stop. And it doesn't sound like anything. No form. No tune. No recognisable references. Holy shit, is he for real? I am completely and utterly floored. My head is spinning. I sink into my seat. And it still doesn't stop. He kept at it for 40 minutes. Without taking the horn from his lips.

The academics applaud. They bloody love it. The bloody know-it-alls. I am shaking. Everything I knew I didn't know has come and smashed me in the face.

There's an interval and I'm ready to run away. But I can't. I'm stuck. I could clear off and catch a set at Ronnie's before the 60 mile drive back to my parents' home in Tiptree, Essex. That would be the sensible thing to do. Perfect antidote to that. But what if the know-it-alls see me go, bailing out like some know-nothing. Fuck it, I'm staying. I'll show them. And let's be honest, the next group have got to be an improvement on the first set.

I couldn't have been more wrong. First off, the leader of the group walks on stage and is wearing a woollen cardigan, a bloody woollen cardigan, on stage. Listen mate, Joe Henderson wouldn't wash his car in a woollen cardigan, let alone appear on stage in one. Good old Andy Sheppard wears a clean cut suit. Why can't you? Then he starts to make some music with the other members of the group.

'Oh come on, this is not helping, what are you guys on?' I am even more angry and confused with this lot. You see, you've got the three of them up there, on stage, but they're not even attempting to play together. They're all over the place. The bass player is trying to dislocate the strings. Has he got something wrong with his fingers? And what is that drummer doing? He's got the oddest assortment of drums and percussion equipment I have ever seen. Yet all he seems capable of doing is scraping any one of his oversized cowbells with a stick. All the while cardigan man is scuttling between various reed instruments, most of which I've never seen before, things I later find out are called sopranino, contrabass clarinet and C-melody saxophone. But all this scuttling results in an equally ear crunching squall.

'Drummer, pleeeeaaaase give us some 4/4,' I'm thinking. Stupid know-nothing kid that I was.

'Bassist, pleeeeaaaase give us a walking line,' I'm thinking. What a fool I was.

This second half goes on even longer than the first and by the end I'm about fit to burst. Cardigan man informs us of the compositions they have just performed. Most of which sound like complex mathematical equations. Then he tells us some of the tunes were standards. Jazz bloody standards? You have got to be kidding.

Oh and what a surprise, the know-it-alls love it. They bloody would, wouldn't they? Especially as there's mathematics involved.

I leave. I can't think because I'm thinking so hard. What? Why? How? Had I really witnessed it? Or was it imagined? Think about it. Think, stupid boy.

It was two years before I heard Evan Parker again. 1991. At Colchester Arts Centre with Eddie Prévost and Rohan De Saram. I had done a lot of thinking in the meantime. Had I caught up? Never. How could you catch up with a man as forward thinking as that? I had, however, caught up with myself. Given myself the time to grow. Fast forward to 2008. I'm still thinking. Hard. We play in the same group now, that's something I would never have imagined 19 years ago. He'll always be 100 years of thinking ahead of me.

On 21 March 1989, nine days after I saw their concert at the Royalty Theatre, Anthony Braxton, Adelhard Roidinger and Tony Oxley made a recording at Maison De La Culture in Amiens. Eventually released as *Seven Compositions (Trio) 1989* by Hat Art, it stands as one of the greatest records in Braxton's discography. It was a short lived group, possibly just this one tour in 1989, but if they ever reformed I would be first in the queue for tickets.

How things change. I even have a woollen cardigan of my own.

Mark Wastell is a UK musician

'I don't see this as the story of a pop group. I see it as the
story of a city,' declares former Factory boss Anthony Wilson
in Grant Gee's Joy Division documentary. 'I remember
Manchester in the mid-70s. It felt like a piece of history that
had been spat out — grimy and dirty.' Cue archive shots of
bomb sites, slum clearances, tower blocks. We're looking
out across a moody, rainsoaked streetscape; off-camera,
someone's talking about collapsing pipes oozing raw sewage
onto the streets of Manchester. The situatedness of Joy
Division: it's become almost a cliche, this idea that the city
explains the music, somehow is the music, and vice versa.
Even at the time, Jon Savage was writing of Joy Division as
'a perfect reflection of Manchester's dark spaces and empty
places: endless sodium lights and semis seen from a speeding
car, vacant industrial sites — the endless detritus of the 19th
century — seen gaping like teeth from an orange bus.'

All of which was entirely lost on me, listening to Joy
Division as a teenager in the sun-drenched, hedonistic
Sydney of 1981. Could there have been two more different
English-speaking cities at that time? Manchester — the
fevered version of Joy Division biographers, in any case —
was a place of heightened tension, of epic post-industrial
decay and upheaval. Sydney, on the other hand, had none
of that urban intensity, no sense of atrophy. Its harbourside
setting is stupendous, but the city itself is a vast suburban
sprawl: relaxed, self-satisfied, somehow too prosaic for
Romantic tragedy. A city lived outwards, not inwards; of the
body, not the mind. The quintessential Sydney experience is
the Zen of the beach: the emptiness, lying still on the sand
as the sun penetrates you, hypnotised by the dull sound
of surf. If there is unease at Sydney's heart, it originates in
this easiness — a sense of life lived on the surface, of hidden
depths ignored.

For all its hedonism, Sydney wasn't yet an international
city in the early 80s. There was a stolid Anglo-Saxon

provincialism about the place, a feeling that real life was elsewhere. From the vantage point of the internet age, it's astonishing how cut off from the world, how information-poor we were. At the height of my Joy Division obsession, I knew nothing about the group, save the defining fact of Ian Curtis's suicide. I had no idea of what Curtis looked like. He remained a disembodied voice, until I eventually came across a small photo accompanying a review of *Still* in one of the three-month-old *NMEs* that occasionally turned up at the newsagent by the wharf where I caught the ferry to school. If Joy Division cultivated their mystique through the art of withholding, the effect was considerably magnified if you lived in Sydney.

Shorn of its context, this music didn't seem like a mirror held up to anything. After all, there are no external references in Curtis's deeply introspective lyrics, no kitchen sink realism. What appealed, in fact, was the opposite of realism — the sheer otherworldliness, untimeliness of Joy Division. It's not that we didn't have our own post-punk in Australia; we did. I was listening to The Birthday Party as well, but it had a bit less of an impact on me. Nick Cave and Mick Harvey were, as I was, private-school boys from the nice suburbs; their brand of *If*-like rebellion was something I could understand too well. And, as John Cage once put it, 'As soon as I understand something, I no longer have any need for it.'

With so little to go on, album artwork was important evidence. *Unknown Pleasures* looked like a print by an uncompromising 70s minimalist (contemporary art being another half-understood fascination). But it was the cover of *Closer*, with its neoclassical graveyard scene, its austere Roman lettering, that made all sorts of connections for me. I was reading Dante's *Inferno*; at school I was studying, in desultory fashion, Book Six of Virgil's *Aeneid*, where Aeneas descends to the underworld and meets his dead lover. I listened to *Closer* on a loop. The more I listened, the more the second side felt like a song cycle: a willed death, a funeral, a glacial underworld descent not of a classical hero, but the modern, existential anti-hero I was reading about in books like Colin Wilson's *The Outsider*.

Looking back now, I recognise in Joy Division a whole aesthetic that formed an escape, a deep fantasy world for me (and, presumably, for Curtis as well). It wasn't post-industrial Manchester: it was a dream version of continental Europe, from which we in the New World in particular had been banished. It was a heady mix of classicism, Romanticism and modernism, all refracted through the pulp culture of art rock and post-punk. If I was getting neoclassicism from Joy Division, then I was also getting Nietzsche from Bowie, constructivism from Kraftwerk, Camus from The Cure. In a way, we intellectually minded teenagers of that time were the last modernists, with our art pop and our Penguin Classics paperbacks; the very last generation that could read a novel by Sartre and still think it might hold the key. Just a few years later Joy Division had turned into New Order, I was studying Communications and reading Barthes, and the paradigm had irrevocably changed.

Now that I live in Northern Europe, I've come full circle. It's Australian hedonism that seems exotic to me. I dream of sunlight and sensuality, the newness of the New World. I don't listen to Joy Division, but I can't deny the music's spectral presence. Camus once wrote about the 'slow trek to rediscover, through the detours of art, those two or three images in whose presence one's heart first opened'. That beguiling image of the underworld journey — to learn secrets only the dead know — is one I've returned to, as recently as in my latest novel, non-coincidentally entitled *Colony*.

Hugo Wilcken is an Australian author

I am at Imperial College, London, with Natasha, a friend
and fellow writer. A, our guide, has led us to the door of what
looks like a meat safe. He explains what to expect once we're
shut in the anechoic chamber. We peer in, size up the space,
its weird moulded geometries — a cubist hedgehog. I will turn
off the fan for complete silence, A says. There's sufficient air
for one person for 15 minutes. Natasha looks nervous so I go
in first. A hands me the end of a long piece of wire, which he
has attached to the light switch. The full effect of the chamber
is best experienced in the dark.

    I had thought that visiting an anechoic chamber might
help me to resolve a problem with my first novel, *The Echo
Chamber*. I was hoping it would get me writing again.
The book is narrated by a woman who believes she has
remarkable powers of hearing, or rather, listening — the
engaged form of hearing. Like an eccentric, solitary R
Murray Schafer, she spends her life accumulating a vast
internal archive of sounds. But in her middle years, where
the book begins, she is going deaf. As her powers of hearing
deteriorate, the distinctions between her sound-memories
become less certain. She decides to write up her past, all the
sounds she's ever heard, before her memories disintegrate
into a squall of white noise.

    Now that A has closed the door, I am alone in the
chamber. The air feels thick. I stand still and allow the dark
to settle around me (it does not come immediately but seems
to grow more intense as the minutes pass). It's hot in here. A
has just killed the testing equipment, which, I notice, emits
a soft, almost musical clicking as the mechanisms cool. Also
audible — in my head — a series of high-pitched notes, like
the effect right after someone has screamed in your ear. I
try to calm this internal sonic pulsing. I'm feeling uneasy,
breathless. I sit on the floor.

    Today, I can't recall exactly how I spent those minutes
in the anechoic chamber. I remember I spoke my name. I

sat very still, felt myself withdraw into myself. At one point I recited 'To A Mouse' ('*Wee, sleekit, cowrin, tim'rous beastie/ O, what a panic's in thy breastie!*'), a poem I'd learnt at school. And my words, which sank, or rose — they seemed to do both — were swallowed up in the strange, heavy air.

The problem I had encountered in writing *The Echo Chamber* related to language and sound. I found it difficult, perhaps impossible, to traduce sound's shifting dynamics, its sheer kinetic energies, into words on the page. I began to realise that words were an inadequate tool to evoke the aural, and from there I started to doubt writing more generally. With two thirds of the book complete, I came to the conclusion that words can at best poorly approximate the truth of experience, and at worst twist it into false shapes. I stopped writing. Instead I listened to music: Schnittke, Schaeffer, Cage. I read Cage. Better to stop writing altogether, I decided, than to soil experience by trying to communicate it in this way, which was, I felt, corrupt or corrupting. I — and by extension my narrator — craved silence.

Now that my ears have adjusted to the change in decibel level, I lie back and try to listen to the silence. Breathe slowly, I tell myself. Calm your heartbeat (which is as audible as it is felt). I feel like a foetus, then, as the air thickens and presses down on me, a corpse. And that is when I hear it: a kind of slow sighing that comes and goes, a high-pitched shifting electrical tone, a bass rumbling — the mechanics of my functioning body. I am experiencing the Cageian epiphany: that true silence does not exist. Later, I will impute this realisation to the narrator of my book and tease out from it the impact of that complex, troubling moment: that however much she craves it, true silence is not possible — because of the din of herself.

When my 15 minutes are up, I get to my feet, follow the wire and switch on the light. I open the door, stunned. I am sightless, groping, like a grub emerging from its pupa. Now it is Natasha's turn. But she has seen the effects on me. What's more, she's sensitive to altered states and fears remaining trapped in them. She's reluctant to enter alone. So I go in with her, tell her to relax, lie down, concentrate on the silence. But once the noise of her nervous breathing settles and becomes distant, she sits up and says, 'I don't like it in here, I feel dead.' I don't tell her she sounds dead. Her voice is dead. We leave the chamber.

A few days after my visit, I returned to my novel and the conundrum of my narrator's desire for silence. Evie needed to rid herself of her memories; I needed to finish writing my book. Put another way, I had to resume writing in order that she, finally, could stop. How to reconcile these opposing compulsions? I thought back to the anechoic chamber. It was possible for Evie to remain silent and complete her story, I realised, only if she came to rely on other people's words. So I decided that Evie would turn to transcription. She would gather letters and diaries and personal papers she'd inherited over the years, and copy them onto her computer.

And that is how the last third of *The Echo Chamber* is constructed. Some of these papers I wrote myself and slotted into the narrative. Others I took from external sources and had Evie transcribe into her story: journals and testimony I'd found in the process of my research. Remembering the experience of being with Natasha in the anechoic chamber, I asked her to write one such section, entries from a diary kept by Evie's only lover, through which the story of their relationship is told. A relationship with a mime artist, who herself aims to exist in silence, and who, in the end, leads Evie to an anechoic chamber, where Evie, like Cage, and like me, is overwhelmed by the sound of herself and the realisation that if silence exists, she cannot be alive to hear it.

Luke Williams is a UK novelist

ROBERT WYATT ON THE GENIUS OF RAY CHARLES
As told to Biba Kopf

Before I can start, there's a caveat... well, two really. One, the conductor Sir Thomas Beecham said that the English don't know much about music but they like the noise it makes. The other is, Gunther Schuller, writing about jazz listeners, talks about the kind of cloth-eared lefties who think that 'Strange Fruit' is a good song. I don't feel I'm an authority on music outside of what I know, there's all kinds of stuff about music I don't understand.

I'd been brought up to believe in serious music. For my dad, most serious was Bartók and Hindemith. He had liked Fats Waller and Duke Ellington before the war, even though he didn't think they were serious music. I did, but my dad knew they were real music at least, and as I was young, they were allowed. By then I was getting as much out of Gil Evans as I was out of Hindemith, and as far as I was concerned it was just as serious. But at that stage I still accepted the idea that there were intrinsically serious and shallow idioms, and my dad's thing was that pop music was intrinsically shallow. I'd heard quite a lot of it because my sister had records, and they didn't interest me a lot. So I didn't have a problem with dad's idea.

Until I came across an LP called *The Genius Of Ray Charles*. I thought: Genius? How could he be a genius if he's only a popular singer? Clearly a misuse of the word. I was like that. I didn't really have any argument with my dad. I really liked my parents and I liked what they liked, the art of the 20th century, the surrealists, the dadaists and all that stuff. But with Ray Charles, it was a difficult moment because as far as I can hear, bearing in mind my caveats, Ray Charles singing a ballad, even a soppy one like 'Don't Let The Sun Catch You Crying', is as good as Bartók's *Violin Concerto* or Miles Davis. I knew it was a slushy pop song, just a tune with tinkly cocktail piano, and because it had violins on it, it didn't have any jazz cred. I couldn't even work out what the words were half the time, but I thought, it's an astonishing record, absolutely beautiful. Suddenly any idea of a hierarchy of art crumbled away in my mind, and as far as I was concerned, there was no intrinsically superior idiom. It was only a small crack in the music listening in the house, but it opened the way for absolutely anything. I could now enjoy Buddy Holly or Beethoven or whatever. After that, I found out I was constantly going against the grain in the sense that every new idiom sets up a hierarchy: good versus naff, quality versus crap, and so on, and on my new trajectory I always seemed to be finding serious, solemn beauty in what was considered naff. Later, when I was making music myself, it was bit embarrassing because we, ie Soft Machine, weren't playing regular pop music. People said, 'This is better than pop music, it is superior.' Once again, I could see incipient hierarchies reemerging, like there was this need to have them.

On *The Genius Of*, one side was big band Ray Charles, 'Let The Good Times Roll', things like that, and the other side was strings. Well, the jazz hierarchy at that time had it that the respectable side was the big band lot, the other side was the girls' stuff, and I always liked the girls' stuff. I went to absurd lengths, it now seems, to break this hierarchy. I was into The Bee Gees, Lynsey De Paul, The Monkees, anything. Gary Glitter? Let it roll. Fantastic. I wasn't just asserting something against an old guard but the very new guard as well, which was very busily constructing an intellectual hierarchy, of which Soft Machine were petty princes. It was completely mad and I thought, I have got to deal with this. So I did a Monkees song.

'Don't Let The Sun Catch You Crying' interested me as well politically. My parents and a lot of their friends on the Left, not revolutionaries, were egalitarian when it came to economic political issues. But in their minds an intellectual aristocracy had replaced the cultural aristocracy that they had relinquished and abandoned. Similarly, as much as the socialist countries abandoned economic hierarchies in the Western sense, they vociferously embraced bourgeois cultural values and had an almost hysterical fear of popular culture. They were taken with a thing called improving music, improving culture, which is good for you, and naff culture, which is bad for you, and children must be guided away from all these bad things. The more I read about it, I realised that this tendency had been going on for centuries. The church, for example, used to have a problem with rabble music. Organised church music was elevating, and the music of the rabble, when they got pissed, caught sexual diseases and that sort of thing, was the bad kind. The church monitored the rabble with totalitarian verve, intervening constantly to break down the power of mob culture and mob music. Following on from that, you couldn't shock my parents' communist or egalitarian friends by saying, 'I don't believe in God', but you could by saying, 'I don't believe in Mozart'.

Well, I really disagreed with that. The Left missed a trick there, because the idea that serious music was morally elevating took a bit of a battering after the Second World War. What they talked about as serious music, basically, was the music of the Austro-Hungarian empire. Opera, symphony and all the great structures of music gave us the Axis powers, and how morally elevating was that? There wasn't anything wrong with the music, but the claims made for it were ersatz religious claims made out of fear of the mob.

All this came out of listening to Ray Charles, who made it perfectly all right to be a genius and I have clung on to that key assertion nervously ever since. Even so, I hadn't yet finished with hierarchies myself. Before buying a record, which wasn't very often in those days, I went on and on subdividing jazz into participants and innovators and geniuses and not-geniuses. All right, we got the geniuses here: Thelonious Monk, yes; Charlie Mingus, yeah; Charlie Parker, yeah; Duke Ellington, John Coltrane, yes... Ornette Coleman, can I buy Ornette Coleman? Well, OK, for the tunes, yeah?

Of course, I was missing the main event, which was hundreds and hundreds of people playing music and having a fantastic time doing it, out of which come some people with a few diamonds. But genius is in the whole culture, fermenting away in hundreds of different ways and every participant is part of it.

Robert Wyatt is a UK singer and songwriter

Rummaging recently through a small box of almost forgotten
mementoes, I discovered an unshelled peanut. The shrivelled
thing was 15 years old, and therefore a less appetising aide
memoire than Proust's madeleine, but it took me back to
1987, when musically speaking, there seemed many choices
one could make, many roads to walk down. On most of them,
however, the end was already in sight; natural culs-de-sac
were built into their design. But, quite unexpectedly, in the
summer of that year a portal opened up a new dimension
outside the mixture of krautrock, Creation Records-style
guitar music, 60s psychedelia and jazz I was blowing my
student grant on at the time.

The annual Edinburgh Fringe Festival is a place where
even an avid culture lover could easily get sated. For three
months, bagpiping buskers, hopeful leafleteers and other
buffoons keep up a self-promotional barrage coaxing you to
an 'entertainment' in a backroom of some pub, abandoned
cinema or out of town aircraft hangar. That summer, I had
been visiting my best friend in Glasgow, and he suggested we
go and stay for a week at his sister's flat in Edinburgh. It so
happened that a girl I was interested in was taking part in a
play up there, making the prospect yet more appealing. As it
turned out, I didn't get the girl, but I did end up with a blown
mind and a handful of nuts.

The Edinburgh Festival is more about art, theatre and
comedy than music, but after an uplifting morning spent at
an exhibition of 19th century death masks, my friends and
I were hungry to hear something by real live human beings.
Fortunately, a handwritten poster pinned to a tree caught
our eye. It is so long ago now that many of the details of the
ensuing six hours have since escaped me. But something
about the billing on that poster encouraged us to seek out
the small church on the outskirts of the city, where a local
contemporary music group — their name long forgotten —
was staging a recital of avant garde works.

The audience was all of 30 strong when we arrived, and half that by the end of the afternoon. The session began with a quadraphonic playback of a spatial musique concrète piece, which slithered around the room like a chain tied to a gekko's tail. This was followed by one of Stockhausen's studies for solo violin. To fully realise it, the players were required to saw the strings intensely enough to cause the bow's horsehairs to snap. But the revelation came with the final piece of the day. At the back of the performance space, the eldest of the troupe, a thick-set, bearded man in his fifties, sat with a small slate and stick of chalk, whispering something under his breath and drawing short chalkmarks. Next to him sat a younger man playing chess with himself. Suddenly we became aware of a scrabbling under our chairs. A third performer was crawling under the rows of seating, occasionally surfacing with a goofy and slightly demented smile before returning to his subterranean wanderings. A woman was randomly dotting the floor with small piles of unshelled peanuts.

Gradually the piece ratcheted up the intensity. The whispering rose to a mutter: an endlessly repeated phrase which sounded something like, 'Itchi-itchi-nili-konichi, Itchi-itchi-nili-konichi...'. The chess player scurried from one end of his board to the other with increasing zest. The human mole was now stumbling over and under furniture, climbing up wall fixtures, rearranging objects like an overwound feng shui droid. And along with several other randomly selected listeners, I had to hold a bunch of peanuts in my outstretched hands.

This was in fact a rendition of one of John Cage's sets of *Variations*. He wrote eight in all between 1958 and 1978, and in hindsight I believe this must have been III or IV, III being for 'any number of people performing any actions', IV requiring 'any number of players, any sounds or combinations of sounds, produced by any means, with or without other activities', as one guide to contemporary music describes them. Out of 60 possible repeated or one-off actions, whoever is planning to perform the piece must determine which ten to carry out by using chance methods such as throwing dice or casting the I Ching. Other chance operations decide their order and duration. It is a perfect, unmusical illustration of one of Cage's many approaches to organisation.

No instruments were played, no mechanical reproductive devices were activated; but somehow the whole mad, dada slapstick genius of the thing generated its own momentum. Determining an event way in advance of its happening, by a formalistic sleight of hand, Cage's trick was to create something he probably wouldn't recognise as his own, should he walk in on it while it was occurring. Dictated by his pre-set instructions, the interlocking surrealistic actions were catalysts in the creation of an entirely unpredictable event. (All this, remember, was before chaos theory had emerged as a popular science.) With authorial presence so ingrained into most discourse on music and art, Cage's gesture was about letting go the ties that too often bind the composer to the public rendition of the work. His piece precluded recourse to an earlier 'authentic' performance, in the same way that is currently applied to Renaissance and Baroque classical music, for example. And, although I was aware of the border-less ambient music proposed by Brian Eno, this was a far purer realisation of the notion that the whole world could be sound, and that a single sonic event could affect the way you heard, visualised and experienced everyday life.

Meanwhile the ballyhoo in front of us was reaching fever pitch. Someone switched on a vacuum cleaner, another flipped on a siren; one half of the chess player's split personality conceded defeat, while its victorious other cleared the board with a sweep of his hand; and the guy at the back was by now screaming 'ITCHI-ITCHI-NILI-KONICHI! ITCHI-ITCHI-NILI-KONICHI!' like a man crying for help as he holds onto a cliff edge with his last finger. I noticed that he had been ticking off each repetition with the chalk, presumably determining the performance's duration with this marker. When at last he couldn't scream any louder, everyone immediately dropped what they were doing and darted into a cupboard. After a decent 30 second pause to make sure the performance had really finished, we dutifully delivered our applause. But nobody re-emerged from the cupboard. It must have been one hell of an aftershow party in there.

I departed with fresh ears and a nut in my pocket.

Rob Young is a UK born music journalist and author

ACKNOWLEDGEMENTS

Thanks to Chris Bohn, Frances Morgan, Mark Pilkington, Reuben Sutherland, Derek Walmsley and Ben Weaver.